I0153145

THE PRESENT STATE OF MUSIC IN FRANCE and ITALY:

OR, The JOURNAL of a TOUR through those Countries, undertaken to collect Materials for A GENERAL HISTORY OF MUSIC.

By CHARLES BURNEY, Mus. D.

Ei cantarono allor si dolcemente,
Che la dolcezza ancor dentro mi suona.

DANTE, Purg. Canto 2do.

LONDON,
Printed for T. BECKET and Co. in the Strand.
MDCCLXXI.

This is a facsimile of Charles Burney's The Present State of Music in France and Italy or, The Journal of a Tour through those Countries. London: Printed for T. Becket and Co. in the Strand, 1771. This was the first edition. A second edition was published in 1773.

Dr. Charles Burney, Mus. D. (1726-1814), organist, composer and music historian.

Music related books written by Dr. Burney include:

1771: The Present State of Music in France and Italy or, The Journal of a Tour through those Countries, undertaken to collect Materials for a General History of Music. London: Printed for T. Becket and Co. (Second edition 1773)

1771: A Letter from the Late Signor Tartini to Signora Maddalena Lombardini (now Signora Sirmen). Published as an Important Lesson to Performers on the Violin. Translated by Dr. Burney. (Also 1779)

1773: The Present State of Music in Germany, the Netherlands, and the United Provinces, or, The Journal of a Tour through those Countries, undertaken to collect Materials for a General History of Music. London: Printed for T. Becket and Co. 2 vols. (Second edition 1775)

1776-1789: A General History of Music from the Earliest Ages to the Present Period, to which is prefixed, a Dissertation on the Music of the Ancients. 4 vols. (Vol 1 reprinted in 1789).

1779: Account of an Infant Musician. [William Crotch.]

1785: An account of Mademoiselle Theresa Paradis.

1785: An Account of the Musical Performances in Westminster-Abbey, and the Pantheon, May 26th, 27th, 29th; and June the 3rd, and 5th, 1784. In Commemoration of Handel.

Standard works on the life of Dr. Burney include:

BURNEY, Frances ['Fanny', Madame d'Arblay, his daughter], Memoirs of Dr. Burney. (1832)

SCHOLES, Percy A.: The Great Dr. Burney: His Life, His Travels, His Works, His Family and His Friends.. (OUP, 1948)

LONSDALE, Roger: Dr. Charles Burney: A Literary Biography: (OUP, 1965)

More information, and fuller bibliography, can also be found in The New Grove Dictionary of Music and Musicians (Macmillan / OUP)

This facsimile is based on digitised camera scanning of the original book, so as to reproduce the original as closely as possible. While efforts are made to reduce distortions, there may be some distortion from the curve in the margin of the original. Any material in colour has been reproduced in black and white. Larger pages, such as inserts, may have been reduced to fit the page size of the facsimile.

Reprinted 2008 Travis & Emery,
17 Cecil Court, London, WC2N 4EZ,
England.
(+44) 20 7240 2129
neworders@travis-and-emery.com

Hardback: ISBN: 1-904331-75-0. ISBN13 978-1-904331-75-9
Paperback: ISBN: 1-904331-76-9. ISBN13 978-1-904331-76-6

THE
PRESENT STATE
OF
MUSIC
IN
FRANCE and ITALY:

OR,

The JOURNAL of a TOUR through those Countries, undertaken to collect Materials for A GENERAL HISTORY OF MUSIC.

By CHARLES BURNEY, Muf. D.

Ei cantarono allor si dolcemente,
Che la dolcezza ancor dentro mi suona.

DANTE, Purg. Canto 2do.

LONDON,
Printed for T. BECKET and Co. in the Strand.
MDCCLXXI.

[It is difficult to write about the arts without uſing terms of art; but though few foreign words, or technical terms, will occur in this Journal, which are not tranſlated or defined the firſt time they are uſed, yet, to ſave the reader the trouble of ſeeking them in the text, or of remembering them, the following are collected and explained here.]

EXPLICATION

OF

Some Musical Terms and Foreign Words, which occur in the following Journal.

ACCADEMIA, a concert.

Adagio, ſlow, in the firſt degree; or, when uſed ſubſtantively, it ſignifies a ſlow movement.

Allegro, gay, or a quick movement.

Appoggiatura, from *appoggiare*, to lean on; a note of embelliſhment; it is uſually written in a ſmall character, as not eſſential to the harmony, though moſt eſſential to melody, taſte, and expreſſion.

Baritono, a voice of low pitch, between a tenor and baſe.

Bravura, as *aria di bravura*, a quick ſong of difficult execution.

Canon, a compoſition in which the parts follow each other in the ſame melody and intervals.

Canto fermo, plain ſong, or chanting in the cathedral ſervice.

Canzone, a ſong.

Contr' Alto, counter-tenor, or a voice of higher pitch than the tenor, but lower than the treble.

Contrapuntiſta, one ſkilled in the laws of harmony, a compoſer.

Contrapunto, counterpoint; compoſition in parts: this term came from the firſt muſic in parts, being expreſſed in points placed over each other.

Dilettante, a gentleman compoſer or performer; ſynonimous with the French word *amateur*.

Diminuendo, diminiſhing a ſound, or rendering it ſofter and ſofter by degrees.

Due Cori, two choirs, orcheſtras, or choruſſes.

Expreſſion, the performing a piece of melody, or a ſingle paſſage, with that energy and feeling which the poetry or paſſion, to be impreſſed upon the hearer, requires.

Forte, loud.

Fugue, a flight and purſuit; a *fugue* differs from a *canon* only in being leſs rigid in its laws; a *canon* is a perpetual *fugue*: the firſt, or leading part gives the law to the reſt in both; but, in the courſe of a *fugue*, it is allowable to introduce epiſodes and new ſubjects.

Funzione, function, ceremony in the church on a feſtival.

Graduale,

Graduale, gradual; an appellation given, in the Romiſh church, to a verſe which is ſung after the epiſtle, and which was anciently ſung on the ſteps of the altar.

Harmony, muſic in parts, in oppoſition to melody.

Imitation, a ſlight ſpecies of *fugue*, in which the parts imitate each other, though not in the ſame intervals, or according to the rigorous laws of a *fugue* or *canon*.

Improvviſatrice, a female who pronounces verſes extempore.

Intermezzo, an interlude, or muſical farce, uſually performed between the acts of a ſerious piece.

Laudiſti, pſalm ſingers.

Maeſtro di Capella, a compoſer, or one who directs a muſical performance in a church or chapel.

Maeſtro del Coro, maſter of the choir.

Melody, an air, or ſingle part, without baſe or accompaniment.

Maſſa Baſſa, a ſilent maſs, whiſpered by the prieſt during a muſical performance.

Mezzo Soprano, a ſecond treble, or voice between the treble and counter-tenor.

Miſerere, the firſt word of the 51ſt Pſalm, in Latin.

Modulation, the art of changing the key, or of conducting the harmony or melody into different keys, in a manner agreeable to the ear, and conformable to eſtabliſhed rules.

Motetto,

Motetto, *Motet*, a Latin hymn, pfalm, or anthem.
Mufico, a general term for mufician; but now chiefly applied in Italy to a *caftrato*.

Offertorio, *Offertory*, an anthem fung, or a voluntary played, at the time the people are making an offering.

Piano, foft.
Plain chant, plain fong, or chanting.
Portamento, conduct of the voice: the *portamento* is faid to be good, when the voice is neither nafal nor guttural.

Ritornello, originally the echo or repetition of any portion of a fong by the inftruments; but, in procefs of time, it became the general term for fymphony, in which fenfe it will be often ufed in this Journal, and which will, perhaps, be called, *Verbum movere loco*; but though the word *Ritornel* is rather obfolete, and has for fome time been fupplied by fymphony, it now wants revival, as fymphony, among modern muficians, is ufually fynonymous with overture.

Saltatori, jumpers, or dancers of uncommon agility.
Siftine, the Pope's chapel is fometimes called the *Siftine* chapel, from Sextus Quintus, who built it.
Soprano, the fupreme, or treble, part in vocal compofitions.

Sostenuto, sustained; or, used substantively, the power of continuing a sound: in this case the harpsichord has no *Sostenuto*, the organ has one.

Steiner, the name of a famous German maker of violins.

Sinfonia, symphony, or overture.

Taste, the adding, diminishing, or changing a melody, or passage, with judgment and propriety, and in such a manner as to *improve* it: if this were rendered an invariable rule in what is commonly called *gracing*, the passages, in compositions of the first class, would seldom be changed.

Virtù, talents, abilities; hence

Virtuoso, a performer.

Voce di Camera, a feeble voice, fit only for a chamber.

Voce di Petto, a voice which comes from the breast, in opposition to one that is nasal or guttural.

Vox Humana, human voice.

THE

INTRODUCTION.

AMONG the numerous accounts of Italy, publiſhed by travellers who have viſited that delightful country, from different motives of intereſt or curioſity; it is ſomewhat exraordinary, that none have hitherto confined their views and reſearches to the riſe and progreſs, or preſent ſtate of muſic in that part of the world, where it has been cultivated with ſuch ſucceſs; and from whence the reſt of Europe has been furniſhed, not only with the moſt eminent compoſers and performers, but even with all its ideas of whatever is elegant and refined in that art.

Not a ſingle picture, ſtatue, or building has been left undeſcribed, or an inſcription uncopied, and yet neither the *Conſervatorios* or muſical ſchools, the *operas*, or the *oratorios*, have ſcarce been mentioned: and though every library is crowded with hiſtories of painting and other arts, as well as with the lives of their moſt illuſtrious profeſſors; muſic and muſicians have been utterly neglected. And this is ſtill the more unaccountable, as no one of the liberal arts is at preſent ſo much cultivated, nor can the Italians now boaſt a ſuperiority over the reſt of Europe in any thing, ſo much as in their muſical productions and performances; for neither their painters, ſculptors, or architects, hiſtorians, poets, or philoſophers of the preſent age, as in ſome centuries paſt, ſo greatly ſurpaſs their cotemporaries on this ſide the Alps, as to excite much curioſity to viſit or converſe with them.

But muſic ſtill *lives* in Italy, while the other arts only ſpeak a *dead language*;

claſſical

classical and learned indeed, but less pleasing and profitable to students than in the days of Leo X. when Italy was perhaps as superior to the rest of the world, and therefore as well worth visiting, as Greece was in the time of Pericles or Alexander.

To say that music was never in such high estimation, or so well understood as it is at present, all over Europe, would be only advancing a fact as evident, as that its inhabitants are now more generally civilized and refined, than in any other period of the history of mankind.

Perhaps the grave and wise may regard music as a frivolous and enervating luxury; but, in its defence, Montesquieu has said that "it is the only one of all the arts which does not corrupt the mind" *. Electricity is universally allowed to be a very entertaining and surprising phenomenon, but it has frequently been la-

* *Esprit des Loix.*

mented that it has never yet, with much certainty, been applied to any useful purpose. The same reflexion has often been made, no doubt, as to music. It is a charming resource, in an idle hour, to the rich and luxurious part of the world. But say the sour and the worldly, what is its use to the rest of mankind? To this it may be answered, that, in England, perhaps more than in any other country, it is easy to point out the humane and important purposes to which it has been applied. Its assistance has been called in by the most respectable profession in this kingdom, in order to open the purses of the affluent for the support of the distressed offspring of their deceased brethren *. Many an orphan is cherished by its influence †.—The pangs of child-birth are softened and rendered less dangerous

* At the *Feast of the Sons of the Clergy.*

† The Messiah is annually performed for the benefit of the *Foundling Hospital.*

and

and dreadful by the effects of its power *. It helps, perhaps, to ſtop the ravages of a diſeaſe which attacks the very ſource of life †. And, laſtly, it enables its own profeſſors to do what few others can boaſt — to maintain their own poor: by that admirable and well-directed inſtitution, known by the name of *The Society for the Support of decayed Muſicians and their Families.*

Muſic has indeed ever been the delight of accompliſhed princes, and the moſt elegant amuſement of polite courts: but at preſent it is ſo combined with things ſacred and important, as well as with our pleaſures, that mankind ſeems wholly unable to ſubſiſt without it: it forms a conſiderable part of divine ſervice in our churches: it is eſſential to military diſcipline; and the theatres would languiſh

* The benefit every year for the *Lying-in Hoſpital*, Brownlow ſtreet.

† The muſical performance for the *Lock Hoſpital.*

without it. Add to this, that there is hardly a private family in a civilized nation without its flute, its fiddle, its harpsichord, or guitar: that it alleviates labour and mitigates pain; and is still a greater blessing to humanity, when it keeps us out of mischief, or blunts the edge of care.

Had the books I have hitherto consulted, which have been very numerous, supplied me with the information I wanted relative to a history of music, upon which I have been long meditating; I should not have undertaken a journey that has been attended with much fatigue, expence, and neglect of other concerns.

But these books are, in general, such faithful copies of each other, that he who reads two or three, has the substance of as many hundred. In hopes, therefore, of stamping on my intended history some marks of originality, or at least of novelty, I determined to allay my thirst of knowledge at the source,

and

and take ſuch draughts in Italy, as England cannot ſupply. It was there I determined to hear with my *own* ears, and to ſee with my *own* eyes; and, if poſſible, to *hear* and *ſee* nothing but *muſic*. Indeed I could have amuſed myſelf agreeably enough in examining pictures, ſtatues, and buildings, but as I could not afford time for all this, without neglecting the chief buſineſs of my journey, I determined not to have " my purpoſe turned awry" by any other curioſity or enquiry *.

With theſe views I left London in the beginning of June 1770, and as I did not intend my work ſhould be local, I determined in the way to Italy to acquire what materials I could relative to the hiſtory of French muſic, as well as to inform

* In the courſe of my journey, however, I was afterwards much pleaſed to find that I could gratify my love for ſculpture and painting even in the purſuit of muſical materials; as it was from theſe I acquired my ideas and drawings of the inſtruments of the ancients as well as of the early moderns.

myſelf of its preſent ſtate. But it would have been both arrogant and unjuſt to have attempted this in the few weeks allowed me to remain in France, had I not before twice viſited Paris, during which time I frequented very much its public places; and for twenty years paſt I had conſtantly been ſupplied with the works of the beſt compoſers, and the writings of the beſt authors on the ſubject of muſic in that kingdom.

THE

PRESENT STATE

OF

MUSIC, &c.

LISLE.

AS I made no confiderable ftop till I reached this city, the capital of French Flanders, I here began my enquiries, and firft tried to difcover the manner of performing the Gregorian chant, which fubfifts throughout France in all cathedrals and collegiate churches. It is oftener performed without the organ than with; and though they have organs in every large church in this town, and throughout the kingdom, I find they are only

only uſed as in our pariſh churches, on Sundays, and on great feſtivals. It appears plainly to me that our old chants and reſponſes were not new compoſitions by Tallis, at the time of the reformation, but only adjuſted to Engliſh words; the little melody they contain being very nearly the ſame as in all catholic churches abroad. It is only on Sundays and feſtivals that parts are added to the *canto fermo* or *plain chant* here. All ſing at other times in uniſon. All the books out of which the prieſts chant, are written upon vellum in the Gregorian note, that is, in the old black lozenge, or ſquare character, upon four lines and ſpaces only. But in order to inform myſelf ſtill further on the ſubject, I found it neceſſary to make myſelf acquainted with M. Devillers, an agreeable and intelligent man in his profeſſion, and organiſt of the principal church here, that of St. Peter. With him I had a long converſation relative to the uſe of *plain chant*. He ſays the boys

are

are taught it by the Gregorian notes, and that no others are uſed by the eccleſiaſtics.

In the French churches there is an inſtrument on each ſide the choir, called the *ſerpent*, from its ſhape, I ſuppoſe, for it undulates like one. This gives the *tone* in chanting, and plays the baſe when they ſing in parts. It is often ill-played, but if judiciouſly uſed, would have a good effect. It is, however, in general overblown, and too powerful for the voices it accompanies; otherwiſe, it mixes with them better than the organ; as it can augment or diminiſh a ſound with more delicacy, and is leſs likely to overpower or deſtroy by a bad temperament, that perfect one, of which the voice only is capable.

The organ in this church is double, and very large, conſiſting of four rows of keys, ſixty four ſtops, and an immenſe front of thirteen columns of pipes: it has been made about ſixty years. The caſe is finely carved and ornamented, and the

front

front pipes of the white and natural colour of the metal, as they are in all the organs here. In England it is neceſſary to gild them, to prevent their turning black. I have always found that but little uſe is made of the organ in France, even on thoſe days when it is moſt employed. The *ſerpent* keeps the voices up their pitch, and is a kind of crutch for them to lean on.

As it was Jubilee-Time * when I was at Liſle, I had hopes of hearing better muſic than ordinary, but was diſappointed.

M. Anneuſe, organiſt of the church of St. Maurice in this town, is blind. I called at his houſe; but he was from home, other-

* The name of jubilee is uſually given to an eccleſiaſtical ſolemnity, or ceremony performed, in order to gain a plenary indulgence from the pope. There are, however, particular jubilees in ſome cities, upon the concurrence of certain feſtivals, as when the feaſt of the Annunciation happens on Good Friday; or that of St. John the Baptiſt, on *Corpus Chriſti* day. Encyclop. Art. Jubilee.

wiſe I would have had ſome converſation with him on the ſubject of his profeſſion. For I found the ſhorteſt and beſt road to ſuch information as I wanted, was to talk with the principal profeſſors, wherever I went. Learned men and books may be more uſeful as to ancient muſic, but it is only *living* muſicians that can explain what *living muſic* is. This method, however, where I had no letters of recommendation, coſt me a little money, ſome aſſurance, and a great deal of trouble.

Thoſe who viſit Italy for the ſake of painting, ſculpture, or architecture, do well to ſee what thoſe arts afford in France, firſt; as they become ſo dainty afterwards, that they can bear to look at but few things that kingdom affords; and as I expected to have the ſame prejudices, or feelings at my return, about their muſic, I endeavoured to give it a fair hearing firſt, in the capital, and the two extremities of the kingdom, Paris, Liſle, and Lyons. I ſtopped at Cambray, viſited

visited the churches there, in hopes of hearing music, but was disappointed; the service was performed entirely without chant or organ. I was told there would be singing in the afternoon, but was unable to stay. Indeed the character given of the voices by some of the inhabitants did not tempt me, so I went on directly to

PARIS.

And here, after spending the greatest part of the first day in search of books, I went in the evening, June 12, to the *Boulevard,* as no better entertainment offered itself either at the play-house or opera. The Boulevard is a place of public diversions, without the gates of Paris. It is laid out in walks, and planted. In the middle is a wide road for carriages, and at the sides are coffee-houses, conjurors, and shows of all kinds. Here every evening, during summer, the walks are crowded with well-dressed people and the road

road with ſplendid equipages; and here I ſaw the new Vauxhall, as they call it, but it is no more like ours, than the emperor of China's palace. Nor is it at all like Ranelagh; though, at the firſt entrance, there is a ſmall rotund, with galleries round it well lighted up, and decorated. Next to this is a quadrangle in the open air, where they dance in warm weather; it is illuminated, and has galleries, which are continued to another room, which is ſquare, and ſtill larger than the firſt, with two rows of corinthian pillars ornamented with feſtoons and illuminations. This is a very elegant room, in which are *minuets*, *allemandes*, *cotillons*, and *contre danſes*, when the weather is cold, which was now the caſe in the extreme. However, here was a great crowd of well-dreſſed people. From the name of this place it was natural to look for a garden, but none was to be found.

In the coffee-houſes on the Boulevard, which are much frequented, there are bands of mufic, and finging, in the Sadler's-Wells way, but worfe. The women who perform there, go about with a plate to collect a reward for their trouble. Here, though they often fing airs *a l' Italienne*, original fin, in the expreffion, fticks as clofe to them as to us, at fuch places, in England.

Wednefday 13. This morning I fpent in the library of the *College Des Quatre nations*, founded by cardinal Mazarin. It is a noble one. I confulted the catalogues, and found feveral of the books I wanted.

In the evening I heard two pieces performed at the *Theatre Italien*, in which the finging was the worft part. Though the modern French compofers hazard every thing that has been attempted by the Italians, yet it is ill executed, and fo ill underftood by the audience, that it makes no impreffion. *Bravura* fongs, or fongs of execution, are now attempted; but

but they are ſo ill performed, that no one uſed to true Italian ſinging can like any thing but the words and action. One of theſe pieces was new, and meant as a comic opera, in all its modern French forms of Italian muſic, (that is, muſic compoſed in the Italian ſtyle) to French words. No recitative, all the dialogue and narrative part being ſpoken. And this piece was as thoroughly d---d as ever piece was here. I uſed to imagine that a French audience durſt not hiſs to the degree I found they did upon this occaſion. Indeed quite as much, mixt with horſe laughs, as ever I heard at Drury Lane, or Covent Garden. In ſhort, it was condemned in all the Engliſh forms, except breaking the benches and the actors heads; and the inceſſant ſound of *hiſh* inſtead of *hiſs*. The author of the words, luckily, or rather judiciouſly, lay concealed; but the compoſer, M. de St. Amant, was very much to be pitied, for a great deal of real good music was thrown away upon bad words, and upon an audience not at all disposed, especially in the two last acts (there were three) to hear any thing fairly. But this music, though I thought it much superiour to the poetry it accompanied, was not without its defects; the modulation was too studied, so much so as to be unnatural, and always to disappoint the ear. The overture however was good music, full of sound harmony, elegant and pleasing melody, with many passages of effect. The hautbois at this theatre is admirable; I hardly ever heard a more pleasing tone or manner of playing. Several of the songs would have been admirable too, if they had been sung with the true Italian expression. But the French voice never comes further than from the throat; there is no *voce di petto*, no true *portamento* or direction of the voice, on any of the stages. And though several of the singers in this theatre

theatre are Italians, they are ſo degenerated ſince they came hither, that if I had not been aſſured of it, their performance would have convinced me of the contrary. The new piece had ſeveral movements in it very like what is heard at the ſerious opera. (It muſt be remembered that the whole was in verſe, and extremely ſerious, except ſome attempt at humour in * Calliot's part) which, however, did not prevent the audience from pronouncing it to be *deteſtable.*

Thurſday 14. This being *Fête Dieu*, or *Corpus Chriſti* Day, one of the greateſt holidays in the whole year, I went to ſee the proceſſions, and to hear high maſs performed at Notre Dame. I had great difficulty to get thither. Coaches are not

* M. Calliot is deſervedly the favourite actor and ſinger of the comic opera at Paris. His voice, which he can make a baſe or a tenor at pleaſure, is admirable, and he is in all reſpects a moſt intereſting and entertaining performer.

allowed to ſtir till all the proceſſions, with which the whole town ſwarms, are over. The ſtreets through which they are to paſs in the way to the churches, are all lined with tapeſtry; or, for want of that, with bed-curtains and old petticoats: I find the better ſort of people, (*les gens comme il faut*) all go out of town on theſe days, to avoid the *embarras* of going to maſs, or the *ennui* of ſtaying at home. Whenever the hoſt ſtops, which frequently happens, the prieſts ſing a pſalm, and all the people fall on their knees in the middle of the ſtreet, whether dirty or clean. I readily complied with this ceremony rather than give offence or become remarkable. Indeed, when I went out, I determined to do as other people did, in the ſtreets and church, otherwiſe I had no buſineſs there; ſo that I found it incumbent on me to kneel down twenty times ere I reached Notre Dame. This I was the leſs hurt at, as I ſaw it quite general;

and many much better dreſſed people than myſelf, almoſt proſtrated themſelves, while I only touched the ground with one knee. At length I reached the church, where I was likewiſe a *conformiſt*; though here I walked about frequently, as I ſaw others do, round the choir and in the great aiſle. I made my remarks on the organ, organiſt, plain-chant, and motets. Though this was ſo great a feſtival, the organ accompanied the choir but little. The chief uſe made of it, was to play over the chant before it was ſung, all through the Pſalms. Upon enquiring of a young abbé, whom I took with me as a *nomenclator*, what this was called? *C'eſt proſer*, 'Tis proſing, he ſaid. And it ſhould ſeem as if our word *proſing* came from this dull and heavy manner of recital. The organ is a good one, but when played full, the echo and reverberation were ſo ſtrong, that it was all confuſion; however, on the choir organ and echo ſtops I could hear every paſſage diſtinctly. The organiſt has a neat and judicious way of touching the inſtrument; but his paſſages were very old faſhioned. Indeed what he played during the *offertorio*, which laſted ſix or eight minutes, ſeemed too ſtiff and regular for a voluntary. Several *motets*, or ſervices, were performed by the choir, but accompanied oftener by the *ſerpent* than organ: though, at my firſt entrance into the French churches, I have frequently taken the *ſerpent* for an organ; but ſoon found it had in its effect ſomething better and ſomething worſe than that inſtrument. Theſe compoſitions are much in the way of our old church ſervices, full of fugues and imitation; more contrivance and labour than melody. I am more and more convinced every day, that what I before obſerved concerning the adapting the Engliſh words to the old *canto fermo*, by Tallis, at the Reformation, is true; and it ſeems to me that muſic, in our cathe-

dral

dral ſervice, was leſs reformed than any other part of the liturgy.

At five o'clock I went to the *Concert Spirituel,* the only public amuſement allowed on theſe great feſtivals. It is a grand concert performed in the great hall of the Louvre, in which the vocal conſiſts of detached pieces of church muſic in Latin *. I ſhall name the ſeveral performances of this concert, and fairly ſay what effect each had upon myſelf, and upon the audience, as far as a ſtander-by could diſcover. The firſt piece was a motet by M. De la Lande, *Dominus regnavit,* chiefly made up of choruſſes, performed with more force than feeling; the whole was in the ſtyle of the old French

* The French have never yet had either a ſerious Italian opera or a regular oratorio of any ſort performed in their country. I ſuppoſe the managers of their public diverſions know too well the taſte of the people to attempt them, though every other ſpecies of novelty is tried, and they even ſuffer Italian to be *ſpoken* by ſeveral of the characters in the Harlequin pieces.

opera ; and, except the ſecond chorus, which had a conduct and ſpirit ſomewhat new and agreeable, to me deteſtable, though much applauded by the audience, who felt and admired it as much as themſelves, for being natives of a country able to produce ſuch maſter-pieces of compoſition, and ſuch exquiſite performers. Then a concerto on the hautbois by Bezzozi, nephew to the celebrated hautbois and baſſoon players of that name at Turin. For the honour of the French, I muſt needs ſay that this piece was very much applauded. It is a ſtep towards reformation, to begin to tolerate what ought to be adopted. This performer has many points in his taſte and expreſſion that are truly exquiſite ; but I think he is not conſtantly perfect. He makes great uſe of his tongue in diviſions, which perhaps occaſions a more frequent crack or cackle in the reed than one would wiſh ; neither is his tone very powerful without forc-

ing,

ing, which, as this was a large room, he perhaps thought neceſſary. Upon the whole, however, I was very much delighted with his performance. But it is not eaſy to account for the latitude the French take in their approbation, or to ſuppoſe it poſſible for people to like things as oppoſite as light and darkneſs. If French muſic is good, and its expreſſion natural and pleaſing, that of Italy muſt be bad: or change the ſuppoſition, and allow that of Italy to be all which an unprejudiced, but cultivated ear could wiſh; the French muſic cannot, one would imagine, give ſuch an ear equal delight. The truth is, the French do not like Italian muſic; they pretend to adopt and admire it; but it is all mere affectation. After this high-finiſhed performance of Bezozzi Mademoiſelle Delcambre ſcreamed out *Exaudi Deus* with all the power of lungs ſhe could muſter; and was as well received as if Bezzozi had done

done nothing. After this Signor Traverſa, firſt violin to the prince de Carignan, played a concerto in the Italian ſtyle very well; many parts with great delicacy, good tone, and facility of execution: but this was not ſo well reliſhed as the *Exaudi* that went before it. Nay, I could plainly diſcover, by their countenances and reception of it, how little they had felt it. Madame Philidor ſung a *motet* next, of her huſband's compoſition, who drinks hard at the Italian fountain; but though this was more like good ſinging and good muſic than any vocal piece that had preceded it, yet it was not applauded with that fury, which leaves not the leaſt doubt of its having been felt. The whole was finiſhed by *Beatus Vir*, a motet, in grand chorus, with ſolo and duet parts between. The principal counter-tenor had a ſolo verſe in it which he bellowed out with as much violence as if he had done it for life, while a knife was at his throat. But though this wholly ſtunned me, I plainly *ſaw*, by the ſmiles of ineffable ſatisfaction which were viſible in the countenances of ninety-nine out of a hundred of the company, and *heard*, by the moſt violent applauſe that a raviſhed audience could beſtow, that it was quite what their hearts felt, and their ſouls loved. *C'eſt ſuperbe!* was echoed from one to the other through the whole houſe. But the laſt chorus was a *finiſher* with a vengeance! it ſurpaſſed, in clamour, all the noiſes I had ever heard in my life. I have frequently thought the choruſſes of our oratorios rather too loud and violent; but, compared with theſe, they are *ſoft muſic*, ſuch as might ſooth and lull to ſleep the heroine of a tragedy.

Friday 15. In viſiting the king of France's library this morning, I found that if I could have contented myſelf

with

with the *dead letter* of information, such as is to be obtained from books only, I need not to have croſſed the Alps; as the number to be found here, relative to my ſubject, is almoſt infinite. The MSS. were what I firſt enquired after of the librarian, and I found that the mere catalogue of theſe alone amounted to four volumes in folio; not all about muſic indeed, but that ſcience has not been neglected by the collectors of theſe books. The moſt ancient MSS. in which muſic has any concern, if we except the ſeven Greek authors publiſhed by Meibomius, which are all here in MS. are the liturgies and offices of the church, ſuch as miſſals, rituals, graduals, breviaries, and pſalters, in Greek and Latin; but of theſe when I come to treat of the muſic of paſt times. Of its preſent ſtate *here*, I thought I could get no better information than was to be acquired by going to the opera of Zaide, which was performed this evening at the new opera-houſe adjoining

ining to, or rather being part of the 'alais *Royal* belonging to the duke of)rleans. The former theatre was burnt own about ſix years ago, during which .me the opera was performed in the .ing's palace of the Louvre, where the 'oncert *Spirituel* is ſtill held *. The pera of to-night was firſt performed in 739; revived again in 1745, 1756, and iow, for the fourth time, in 1770. I s called by the French *ballet-heroique*, o ieroic dance; the dances being inter woven, and making an eſſential part c the piece. I believe in all ſuch pieces, th intereſt of the drama is very inconſider able; at leaſt, if we may judge by thi and ſome of thoſe compoſed by Rameau

* One of the fineſt ſights at Paris uſed then be the Tuilleries in ſummer, after the opera; whi being over between ſeven and eight in the evenin all the company, in full dreſs, conſiſting of t flower of this capital, poured into the grand av nue: *totis vomit Ædibus undam*; and formed aſſembly not to be met with in any other part the world.

T!

The music of Zaide is by Royer; and it is somewhat wonderful that nothing better, or of a more modern taste, has been composed since; the style of composition is totally changed throughout the rest of Europe; yet the French, commonly accused of more levity and caprice than their neighbours, have stood still in music for thirty or forty years: nay, one may go still further, and assert boldly, that it has undergone few changes at the great opera since Lulli's time, that is to say, in one hundred years. In short, notwithstanding they can both talk and write so well, and so much *about it*, music in France, with respect to the two great essentials of melody and expression *, may still be said to be in its infancy.

But to return to M. Royer's *opera* of Zaide, which, in point of melody, of light and shade, or contrast, and of effect,

* The Italian music, says M. D'Alembert, is a language of which we have not yet the alphabet.
Melange de Litter.

is miſerable, and below all criticiſm: but at the ſame time it muſt be allowed that the theatre is elegant and noble; that the dreſſes and decorations are fine; the machinery ingenious; and the dancing excellent: but, alas! theſe are all objects for the eye, and an opera elſewhere is intended to flatter the ear. A muſical drama, which has nothing intereſting in the words, and of which the muſic is bad, and the ſinging worſe, muſt ſurely fall ſhort of every idea that has been formed in other countries of ſuch a ſpecies of exhibition.

Three out of five of the principal ſingers in Zaide, I had heard at the *Concert Spirituel.* Meſſieurs Gelin and Le Gros, and Mademoiſelle du Bois; the other two were M. and Mad. L'Arrivée; in their manner of ſinging much like the reſt. One thing I find here, which makes me grieve at the abuſe of nature's bounty, the voices are in themſelves really good and well toned; and this is eaſily to be diſcovered,

covered, in despight of false direction and a vitiated expression. But of this enough has already been said: a word or two more about their composition, and I have done with their music for some time; at least with their expression: for they have some composers of great merit among them, who imitate very successfully the Italian style. But it is in vain, at least for the natives of France; other nations may indeed be the better for it; but let this detestable and unnatural expression be given to any music in the world, and it becomes immediately French. One may apply to French singers, what Dryden said of Mac Flecno's wit—

> *Sound* pass'd thro' them no longer is the same,
> As food digested takes a different name.

But it seems to be with the serious French opera here, as it is with our oratorios in England; people are tired of the old by hearing them so often; the style has been pushed perhaps to its utmost boundary,

dary, and is exhausted; and yet they cannot relish any new attempts at pleasing them in a different way: what is there in this world not subject to change? And shall we expect music to be permanent above *all* things, which so much depends on imagination and feeling?

There are particular periods, that one would perhaps wish to stop at, if it were possible; but as that cannot be, let us comply with necessity, in good humour, and with a good grace. Poetry, painting, and sculpture have had their rise and declension: have sunk into barbarism: have emerged from it in succeeding ages, and mounted to a certain degree of perfection, from which they have gradually and insensibly sunk again to the lowest state of depravity: and yet these arts have a standard in the remains of antiquity, which music cannot boast. There are classicks in poetry, sculpture, and architecture, which every modern strives to imitate; and he is thought moſt to excel, who comes neareſt to thoſe models. But who will venture to ſay, that the muſician who ſhould compoſe or perform like Orpheus, or Amphion, would be deſervedly moſt applauded now? Or who will be bold enough to ſay, *how* theſe immortal bards *did* play and ſing, when not a ſingle veſtige of their muſic, at leaſt that is intelligible to us, remains? As far as we are able to judge, by a comparative view of the moſt ancient muſic with the modern, we ſhould gain nothing by imitation. To copy the *canto fermo* of the Greek church, or that of the Roman ritual, the moſt ancient muſic now ſubſiſting, would be to retreat, not to advance in the ſcience of ſound, or arts of taſte and expreſſion. It would afford but ſmall amuſement to ears acquainted with modern harmony, joined to modern melody. In ſhort, to ſtop the world in its motion is no eaſy taſk; on we *muſt* go, and he that lags behind is but loſing time, which it will coſt him much labour to recover.

Indeed many of the firſt perſons in France, for genius and taſte, give up the point: among whom are Meſſieurs Diderot, D'Alembert, and the Abbé Arnaud. Meſſieurs De la Lande and De Blainville openly rank on the Italian ſide likewiſe; but it ſeems always with ſome degree of reſerve: (ſee M. De la Lande, *Voyage d'un François*, p. 224, tom. vi.) they ſtill lay great ſtreſs on dancing and decoration; but how few ſubjects fit for muſic will admit dancing in the texture of the drama? And as to ſinging and dancing at the ſame time, if equally good, they muſt diſtract and divide the attention in ſuch a manner as to make it impoſſible to enjoy either: it would be eating of two coſtly diſhes, or drinking of two exquiſite wines at once—they reciprocally deſtroy the effect of each other. When muſic is really good, and well performed, the hearer of taſte wants no adjunct or additional provocative to ſtimulate attention.

Sunday. I went to St. Rocque, to hear the celebrated M. Balbaſtre, organiſt of that church, as well as of Notre Dame and the Concert Spirituel *. I had ſent the day before to enquire when M. Balbaſtre would play, as a ſtranger from England was very curious to hear him. He was ſo obliging as to ſay he ſhould be glad to ſee me at his houſe, or would attend me at St. Roque, between three and four o'clock.—I preferred the latter, as I thought it would give him leaſt trouble, ſuppoſing he would, of courſe, be at church, but I found he was not expected; and that it was in complaiſance that he came. He very politely took me up into the organ-loft with him, where I could ſee as well as hear. The organ

* There are four organiſts of Notre Dame, who play quarterly — Meſſieurs Couperin, Balbaſtre, D'Aquin, and Fouquet.

is an immenſe inſtrument, made not above twenty years ago; it has four ſets of keys, with pedals; the great and choir organ communicate by a ſpring: the third row of keys is for the reed ſtops, and the upper for the echoes. This inſtrument has a very good effect below; but above the keys are intolerably noiſy. M. Balbaſtre took a great deal of pains to entertain me; he performed in all ſtyles in accompanying the choir. When the *Magnificat* was ſung, he played likewiſe between each verſe ſeveral minutes, fugues, imitations, and every ſpecies of muſic, even to hunting pieces and jigs, without ſurpriſing or offending the congregation, as far as I was able to diſcover. In *proſing*, I perceived he performed the chant on the pedals, which he doubled with the loweſt part of the left hand, and upon this baſis played with learning and fancy. The baſe part was written in ſemibreves, like our old pſalmody. What was ſung in the choir, without the organ, was inſerted in the Gregorian character.

After church M. Balbaſtre invited me to his houſe, to ſee a fine Rucker harpſichord which he has had painted inſide and out with as much delicacy as the fineſt coach or even ſnuff-box I ever ſaw at Paris. On the outſide is the birth of Venus; and on the inſide of the cover the ſtory of Rameau's moſt famous opera, Caſtor and Pollux; earth, hell, and elyſium are there repreſented: in elyſium, ſitting on a bank, with a lyre in his hand, is that celebrated compoſer himſelf; the portrait is very like, for I ſaw Rameau in 1764. The tone of this inſtrument is more delicate than powerful; one of the uniſons is of buff, but very ſweet and agreeable; the touch very light, owing to the quilling, which in France is always weak.

M. Balbaſtre had in the ſame room a very large organ, with pedals, which it

may

may be neceſſary for a French organiſt to have for practice; it is too large and coarſe for a chamber, and the keys are as noiſy as thoſe at St. Roque. However M. Balbaſtre did his beſt to entertain and oblige me, and I had great reaſon to be ſatisfied both with his politeneſs and performance.

Monday 18. This evening I went to St. Gervais, to hear M. Couperin, nephew to the famous Couperin, organiſt to Louis XIV. and to the regent duke of Orleans; it being the vigil or eve of the Feaſt of Dedication, there was a full congregation. I met M. Balbaſtre and his family there; and I find this annual feſtival is the time for the organiſts to diſplay their talents. M. Couperin accompanied the *Te Deum*, which was only chanted, with great abilities. The interludes between each verſe were admirable. Great variety of ſtops and ſtyle, with much learning and knowledge of the inſtrument, were ſhewn, and a finger equal in ſtrength and rapidity to every difficulty. Many things of effect were produced by the two hands, up in the treble, while the baſe was played on the pedals.

M. Balbaſtre introduced me to M. Couperin, after the ſervice was over, and I was glad to ſee two eminent men of the ſame profeſſion, ſo candid and friendly together. M. Couperin ſeems to be between forty and fifty; and his taſte is not quite ſo modern, perhaps, as it might be; but allowance made for his time of life, for the taſte of his nation, and for the changes muſic has undergone elſewhere, ſince his youth, he is an excellent organiſt; brilliant in execution, varied in his melodies, and maſterly in his modulation.

It is much to be wiſhed that ſome opportunity, like this annual meeting, were given in England to our organiſts, who have talents, and good inſtruments to diſplay. It would awaken emulation,

and

and be a ſtimulus to genius; the performer would be ſure of being well heard, and the congregation well entertained.

The organ of St. Gervais, which ſeems to be a very good one, is almoſt new; it was made by the ſame builder, M. Cliquard, as that of St. Rocque. The pedals have three octaves in compaſs; the tone of the loud organ is rich, full, and pleaſing, when the movement is ſlow; but in quick paſſages, ſuch is the reverberation in theſe large buildings, every thing is indiſtinct and confuſed. Great latitude is allowed to the performer in theſe interludes; nothing is too light or too grave, all ſtyles are admitted; and though M. Couperin has the true organ touch, ſmooth and connected; yet he often tried, and not unſucceſsfully, mere harpſichord paſſages, ſmartly articulated, and the notes detached and ſeparated.

Tueſday, July 19. Was ſpent in the king's library.

Wedneſday

Wednesday 20. I heard M. Pagin on the violin, at the houſe of Mad. Brillon, at Paſſy; ſhe is one of the greateſt lady-players on the harpſichord in Europe. This lady not only plays the moſt difficult pieces with great preciſion, taſte, and feeling, but is an excellent ſight's-woman; of which I was convinced by her manner of executing ſome of my own muſic, that I had the honour of preſenting to her. She likewiſe compoſes; and was ſo obliging as to play ſeveral of her own ſonatas, both on the harpſichord and *piano forte*, accompanied on the violin by M. Pagin. But her application and talents are not confined to the harpſichord; ſhe plays on ſeveral inſtruments; knows the genius of all that are in common uſe, which ſhe ſaid it was neceſſary for her to do, in order to avoid compoſing for them ſuch things as were either impracticable or unnatural; ſhe likewiſe draws well and engraves, and is a moſt accompliſhed and agreeable woman. To this

this lady many of the famous composers of Italy and Germany, who have resided in France any time, have dedicated their works; among these are Schobert and Boccherini.

M. Pagin was a pupil of Tartini, and is regarded here as his best scholar; he has a great deal of expression and facility of executing difficulties; but whether he did not exert himself, as the room was not large, or from whatever cause it proceeded, I know not, his tone was not powerful. Music is now no longer his profession; he has a place under the Compte de Clermont, of about two hundred and fifty pounds sterling a year. He had the *honour* of being hissed at the *Concert Spirituel* for daring to play in the Italian style, and this was the reason of his quitting the profession.

Thursday. I had the honour of being introduced to the acquaintance of M. L'Abbé Arnaud, of the Academy Royal *des Inscriptions et Belles Lettres*; his conversation

ſation confirmed what I had gathered from his writings, that he was not only a man of great learning, but of great taſte. His diſſertation upon the accents of the Greek tongue is both ingenious and profound; there is a truth and preciſion in his ideas concerning the arts, which are irreſiſtible to a mind at all open to conviction. With this gentleman I had the honour to diſcuſs ſeveral points relative to the muſic of the ancients, and the happineſs of being confirmed in ſome opinions I had already formed, and enlightened in others.

At the *Comedie Françoiſe* I was this night very much entertained by the repreſentation of *La Surpriſe d'Amour*, and *George Dandin*; the former is a piece of Marivaux, and was admirably played; the latter is Moliere's, and a mere farce, full of buffoonery and indecency: it is with this piece, as with ſome of Shakeſpeare's, the name ſupports it; for was any modern writer to produce ſuch

groſs

groſs ribaldry and nonſenſe, it would be very ſhort-lived: at the ſame time it muſt be confeſſed, that here and there, as in Shakeſpeare's worſt pieces, there are ſtrokes of genius and ſtrong comic wit that ought to live for ever. Preville played admirably a clown's part in both theſe comedies; his humour is always eaſy and natural, and there is a perpetual laugh runs through the houſe from the time he enters, till he quits the ſtage. I perceive that the overtures and act tunes of this theatre, as of the *Theatre Italien*, are all either German or Italian; they begin to be aſhamed of their own muſic every where but at the ſerious opera; and this revolution in their ſentiments ſeems to have been brought about by M. Rouſſeau's excellent *Lettre ſur la Muſique Françoiſe*.

Friday. I met to-day with M. L'Abbé Rouſſier; had a long converſation with him relative to ancient muſic; his *Memoire*

Memoire upon that ſubject, juſt publiſhed, has gained him great reputation here. He ſeems to have diſcovered, in the *Triple Progreſſion*, the true foundation of all the Greek Syſtems *. I undertook, at his requeſt, to carry two of his books to Bologna, one for *Padre Martini*, and one for the *Inſtitute*.

At dinner to-day I again met with M. L'Abbé Arnaud; M. Gretry, and the famous Liotard, the painter of Geneva, were of the party. M. Gretry, the beſt, and, at preſent, the moſt faſhionable compoſer of the comic opera, has lived eight years in Italy, and is author of *Lucile*, *Le Tableau parlant*, and the *Huron*; all pieces that have had great ſucceſs, how deſervedly I do not pretend to ſay, not having either heard or ſeen them; but from the character given them, by perſons of good taſte and ſound judgment, I expect them to be excellent: the author is a young

* Memoire ſur la Muſique des Anciens, Paris, 1770.

man, and in appearance and behaviour very agreeable; he requeſted me to be the bearer of a letter to *Padre Martini*, under whom he ſtudied ſome time at Bologna.

It may not be amiſs to remark here, that in converſation with M. Gretry, a young Lyric compoſer, about the poems he had to ſet, he agreed with me entirely in my aſſertion, that there were in France, and elſewhere, men, at preſent, who wrote very pretty verſes, full of wit, invention, and paſſion; admirable to read, but very ill calculated for ſong; and perhaps one may venture to ſay, that, among all the ingenious and elegant writers of this age, Metaſtaſio is the beſt and almoſt the only *Lyric Poet* *.

A ſong for muſic ſhould conſiſt only of one *ſubject* or *paſſion*, expreſſed in as *few* and as *ſoft words as poſſible*. Since the refinement of melody, and the excluſion of recitative, a ſong, which uſually recapitulates,

* By Lyric Poet is here meant one who writes poems for muſic.

lates, illuſtrates, or cloſes a ſcene, is not the place for epigrammatic points, or for a number of heterogeneous thoughts and claſhing metaphors; if the writer has the leaſt pity for the compoſer, or love for muſic, or wiſhes to afford the leaſt opportunity for ſymmetry in the air, in his ſong, I ſay again, the thought ſhould be *one*, and the expreſſion as eaſy and laconic as poſſible: but, in general, every new line in our ſongs introduces a new thought; ſo that if the compoſer is more tender of the poet's reputation than of his own, he muſt, at every line, change his ſubject, or be at ſtrife with the poet; and, in either caſe, the alternative is intolerable.

In an air, it is by reiterated ſtrokes that paſſion is impreſſed; and the moſt paſſionate of all muſic is, perhaps, that where a beautiful paſſage is repeated, and where the firſt ſubject is judiciouſly returned to, while it ſtill vibrates on the ear, and is recent in the memory: this, no doubt, may

may be, and often is, carried too far; but not by men of true genius and taſte.

At night, juſt before my departure from Paris, I went to the Italian theatre, to hear *On ne s'aviſe jamais de tout*, and *Le Huron*. The *Huron* is an entertaining drama, taken from M. de Voltaire's *Ingenu*; the muſic by M. Gretry, in which there are many pretty and ingenious things, wholly in the *buon guſto* of Italy; which convinced me, that this compoſer had not been eight years in that country for nothing. But I could not help remarking that our young compoſers, who are profeſſed imitators of Italian muſic, though they have never been in Italy, leſs frequently deviate into abſolute Engliſh muſic, than M. Gretry into French; for ſeveral of his melodies are wholly French: but it ſeems not difficult to account for this; in France there are no genuine Italian operas, either ſerious or comic; ſo that England, where we have both in great perfection, in the Italian language, compoſed and performed by Italians, may be ſaid to be a better ſchool for a young compoſer than France; at leaſt his taſte, if already formed upon that of Italy, is leſs likely to be vitiated and depraved in a country where good ſinging may frequently be heard, than in one where it is hardly too much to ſay, it is *never* to be heard at the theatres.

LYONS.

From the vicinity of this place to Italy, it was natural to ſuppoſe that the muſic here would have been tinctured rather more by the Italian *guſto* than at Paris; but, on the contrary, what is bad at Paris, is worſe here. At the theatre, which is a very pretty one, the ſinging is deteſtable: I was entertained however at a coffee-houſe by an Italian family, who, I am certain, were never heard in Italy but in the ſtreets, yet here their performance was charming.

The

The father played the firft violin, and with great fpirit; the fecond violin, and the violoncello were played by his two fons; and the vocal part was performed by his two daughters, who fung airs and duets by turns. Nothing was demanded by the landlady, but for the coffee and other things that were drank; but the girls, after each fong, went about the room with a plate, to collect what the generofity of each new comer would afford; which, I fear, was but little, if one may judge by the attention to the mufic; for fuch an inceffant chattering I never heard among the moft loquacious female goffips, as the company, not the *audience*, here made, during the prettieft airs that were either fung or played.

The firft violin of this town is an old Venetian, Signor Carminati, one of Tartini's earlieft fcholars. And the principal performer on the harpfichord, Signor Leoni; but both have been here long enough to have accommodated themſelves to the muſic and taſte of this country.

I went twice to the cathedral church of St. John, to hear the *Plain Chant à la Romaine*, and found both the church and the muſic as plain and unadorned with pictures, ſtatues, harmony, or taſte, as any proteſtant church I ever was in. The prebends, who are here called counts, the canons, and twenty-four boys, all ſing in uniſon, and without organ or books.

GENEVA.

There is but little muſic to be heard in this place, as there is no play-houſe allowed; nor are there organs in the churches, except two, which are uſed for pſalmody only, in the true purity of John Calvin: however, M. Fritz, a good compoſer, and excellent performer, on the violin, is ſtill living; he has reſided here near thirty years, and is well known to all the Engliſh lovers of muſic who have viſited Geneva during that time. In his youth he had ſtudied under Somis, at Turin.

Turin. It was rather awkward to go to him; but I ſent a meſſage over night, and he appointed two o'clock the next day. He lives at a houſe about a mile out of town. I found him to be a thin, ſenſible looking old man, and we ſoon grew very well acquainted. He was ſo obliging as to play me one of his own ſolos, which, though extremely difficult, was pleaſing; and though he muſt be near ſeventy years of age, he ſtill performs with as much ſpirit as a young man of twenty-five. His bowing and expreſſion are admirable; and he muſt himſelf be a *real lover* of muſic to keep in ſuch high practice, with ſo few opportunities of diſplaying his talents, or of receiving their due reward. He is on the point of publiſhing, by ſubſcription, ſix ſymphonies.*

Beſides M. Fritz, on the practical ſide, Geneva can boaſt an excellent theoriſt,

* This excellent performer, when at Paris, ſome years ago, had the ſame honours conferred upon him at the *Concert Spirituel* as M. Pagin. (See p. 39.)

M. Serre, an eminent miniature painter, who has written ſome learned and ingenious eſſays on the theory of harmony. I had the pleaſure of converſing with him on the ſubject, and of communicating to him the plan of my intended hiſtory of muſic. He is thought to be very deep in the ſcience of ſound: ſeemed pleaſed with my viſit, and returned it the ſame evening; entering very heartily into my views, and ſeeming ſolicitous that I ſhould purſue them.

My going to M. Fritz, broke into a plan I had formed of viſiting M. de Voltaire at the ſame hour, with ſome other ſtrangers, who were then going to Ferney. But, to ſay the truth, beſides the viſit to M. Fritz being more *my buſineſs*, I did not much like going with theſe people, who had only a bookſeller to introduce them; and I had heard that ſome Engliſh had lately met with a rebuff from M. de Voltaire, by going without any letter of recommendation, or any thing

thing to recommend themſelves. He aſked them what they wanted? Upon their replying they wiſhed only to ſee ſo extraordinary a man, he ſaid—"Well, "gentlemen, you now ſee me—did you "take me for a wild beaſt or monſter, "that was fit only to be ſtared at as "a ſhow?" This ſtory very much frighted me; for not having any intention of going to Geneva, when I left London, or even Paris, I was quite unprovided with a recommendation: however I was determined to ſee his place, (which I took to be—

Cette maiſon d'Ariſtippe, ces jardins d' Epicure:

to which he retired in 1755, but was miſtaken.) I drove to it alone, after I had left M. Fritz. His houſe is three or four miles from Geneva, but near the lake. I approached it with reverence, and a curioſity of the moſt minute kind. I enquired *when* I firſt trod on his domain; I had an intelligent and talkative poſtillion, who anſwered all my queſtions very ſatisfactorily. His eſtate is very large here, and he is building pretty farm-houſes upon it. He has erected on the Geneva ſide a quadrangular *juſtice*, or gallows, to ſhew that he is the *ſeigneur*. One of his farms, or rather manufacturing houſes (for he is eſtabliſhing a manufacture upon his eſtate) was ſo handſome that I thought it was his *chateau*. We drove to Ferney, through a charming country, covered with corn and vines, in view of the lake and mountains of Gex, Swiſſerland, and Savoy. On the left hand, approaching the houſe, is a neat chapel with this inſcription:

DEO
EREXIT
VOLTAIRE.
M DCC LXI.*

* When this building was conſtructed, M. de Voltaire gave a curious reaſon for placing upon it this inſcription. He ſaid that it was high time to dedicate *one church to God*, after ſo many had been dedicated to Saints.

I ſent

I ſent to enquire whether a ſtranger might be allowed to ſee the houſe and gardens, and was anſwered in the affirmative. A ſervant ſoon came, and conducted me into the cabinet or cloſet where his maſter had juſt been writing, which is never ſhewn when he is at home; but having walked out, I was allowed that privilege. From thence I paſſed to the library, which is not a very large one, but well filled. Here I found a whole length figure in marble of himſelf, recumbent, in one of the windows; and many curioſities in another room; a buſt of himſelf, made not two years ſince; his mother's picture; that of his niece, Mad. Denis; his brother, M. Dupuis; the Calas family, and others. It is a very neat and elegant houſe, not large, or affectedly decorated. I ſhould have ſaid, that cloſe to the chapel, between that and the houſe, is the theatre, which he built ſome years ago; where he treated his friends with ſome of his own tragedies: it it is now only uſed as a receptacle for wood and lumber, there having been no play acted in it theſe four years. The ſervant told me his maſter was ſeventy-eight, but very well. "*Il travaille,*" ſaid he "*pendant dix heures chaque jour.*" He ſtudies ten hours every day; writes conſtantly without ſpectacles, and walks out with only a domeſtic, often a mile or two—"*Et le voila, là bas!*"—and ſee, yonder where he is.—

He was going to his workmen. My heart leaped at the ſight of ſo extraordinary a man. He had juſt then quitted his garden, and was croſſing the court before his houſe. Seeing my chaiſe, and me on the point of mounting it, he made a ſign to his ſervant, who had been my *Cicerone,* to go to him, in order, I ſuppoſe, to enquire who I was. After they had exchanged a few words together, he approached the place where I ſtood, motionleſs, in order to contemplate his perſon as much as I could when his eyes were

turned

turned from me; but on feeing him move towards me, I found myfelf drawn by fome irrefiftible power towards him; and, without knowing what I did, I infenfibly met him half way. It is not eafy to conceive it poffible for life to fubfift in a form fo nearly compofed of mere fkin and bone, as that of M. de Voltaire. He complained of decrepitude, and faid he fuppofed I was curious to form an idea of the figure of one walking after death. However his eyes and whole countenance are ftill full of fire; and though fo emaciated, a more lively expreffion cannot be imagined. He enquired after Englifh news, and obferved that poetical fquabbles had given way to political ones; but feemed to think the fpirit of oppofition as neceffary in poetry as in politics. "*Les querelles d'auteurs font pour le bien de la littérature, comme dans un governement libre, les quarelles des grands, et les clameurs des petits font neceffaires* *ſaires a la liberté.*" * And added, "When critics are ſilent, it does not ſo much prove the age to be correct as dull." He enquired what poets we had now; and I told him we had Maſon and Gray. They write but little, ſaid he, and you ſeem to have no one who lords it over the reſt like Dryden, Pope, and Swift. I told him that it was, perhaps, one of the inconveniencies of periodical journals, however well executed, that they often ſilenced modeſt men of genius, while impudent blockheads were impenetrable, and unable to feel the critic's ſcourge: that Mr. Gray and Mr. Maſon had both been illiberally treated by mechanical critics, even in news-papers; and added, that modeſty and love of quiet ſeemed in theſe gentlemen to have got the better even of their love of fame. During this

* Diſputes among authors are of uſe to literature; as the quarrels of the great, and the clamours of the little, in a free government, are neceſſary to liberty.

con-

conversation, we approached the buildings he was constructing near the road to his *chateau*. These, said he, pointing to them, are the most innocent, and, perhaps, the most useful of all my works. I observed that he had other works, which were of far more extensive use, and would be much more durable than those. He was so obliging as to shew me several farm-houses he had built, and the plans of others; after which I took my leave, for fear of breaking in upon his time, being unwilling to rob the public of things so precious as the few remaining moments of this great and universal genius.

TURIN.

At the first entrance into Italy, if the entertainment were as good as at Rome or Naples, travellers would be inclined to stop short; but they find the curiosities, both of art and nature, still more numerous and interesting the nearer they approach those capitals.

Turin is, however, a very beautiful city, though inferior perhaps to many others in antiquities, natural curiofities, and in the number of its artifts.

The language here is half French and half Italian, but both corrupted. This cannot be applied to the mufic, for Turin has produced a Giardini; and there are at prefent in this city the famous *Dilettante*, Count Benevento, a great performer on the violin, and a good compofer; the two Bezozzi's, and Pugnani; all, except the Count, in the fervice of the King of Sardinia. Their falary is not much above eighty guineas a year each, for attending the chapel royal; but then the fervice is made very eafy to them, as they only perform folos there, and thofe juft when they pleafe. The *Maeftro di Capella* is Don Quirico Gafparini. In the chapel there is commonly a fymphony played every morning, between eleven and twelve o'clock, by the king's band, which is divided into three orcheftras, and placed

placed in three different galleries; and though far ſeparated from each other, the performers know their buſineſs ſo well that there is no want of a perſon to beat time, as in the opera and *concert ſpirituel* at Paris. The king, the royal family, and the whole city ſeem very conſtant in their attendance at maſs; and all their devotion is ſilently performed at the *Meſſa Baſſa*, during the ſymphony *. On feſtivals Signor Pugnani, or the Bezozzis play a ſolo, and ſometimes motets are performed with voices. The organ is in the gallery which faces the king, and in this ſtands the principal firſt violin.

The ſerious opera begins here the ſixth of January, the king's name-day, and continues every day, except Friday, till Lent, and this is called the *Carnival*. Here is an excellent tenor voice, Signor

* The morning ſervice of the church here is called *Meſſa Baſſa*, when the prieſt performs it in a voice ſo little louder than a whiſper, that it cannot be heard through the inſtruments.

Ottane, who ſings with taſte, and in a pleaſing manner. He favoured me with two or three airs, in different ſtyles, which diſcovered him to be a maſter of his profeſſion. He likewiſe paints well, in the manner of Claude Lorrain and Du Vernet, and is ſometimes employed as a painter by his Sardinian majeſty. In October a company of burletta performers comes hither, and remains till Chriſtmas, at the little theatre, where there is, during ſummer, a company of *buffo* comedians, which exhibits every night, except Friday, *una farſa fatta da ridere*, and an *intermezzo in muſica a quattro voci.* * This continues till the burlettas begin. I went thither the evening after my arrival; there was not much company; the boxes, or *palchetti*, are all engaged by the year, ſo that ſtrangers have no place but in the pit; which, however, is far more comfortable than the *parterre* or

* A farce to laugh at, and a muſical interlude for four voices.

pit,

pit, at Paris, where the company ſtand the whole time; and even than that at London, where they are much crowded; but there are backs to the benches in this theatre, which are of double uſe, as they keep off the crowd behind, and ſupport thoſe who fill them. This theatre is not ſo large as that at Lyons, but pretty, and capable of holding much company: it is *diſlungato,* or of an oblong form, with the corners rounded off. There are no galleries in it, but then there are five rows of boxes, one above another, twenty-four in each row; and each box will contain ſix perſons, amounting in all to ſeven hundred and twenty; there is one ſtage-box only on each ſide. The farce was truly what it promiſed, except the laughing part, as it did not produce that effect. The *intermezzo* was not bad; the muſic pretty, but old; the ſinging very indifferent for Italy, though it would have been very good in France. However, it is but juſt to ſay, that, as a drama, the French comic operas have greatly the advantage over the Italian; take away the muſic from the French, and they would be ſtill pretty comedies; but, without muſic, the Italian would be inſupportable. There were four characters; the two girls were juſt not offenſive. Of the men ſo much cannot be ſaid: none of them would have pleaſed in London; and the Italians themſelves hold theſe performances in no very high eſtimation: they talk the whole time, and ſeldom attend to any thing but one or two favourite airs, during the whole piece: * the only two that were applauded were encored; and I obſerved, that the performer does not take it as ſuch a great favour to be applauded here as in England; where, whenever a hand is moved, all illuſion is deſtroyed by a bow or a

* I ſhall have frequent occaſion to mention the noiſe and inattention at the muſical exhibitions in Italy; but muſic there is cheap and common, whereas in England it is a coſtly exotic, and more highly prized.

curtſey

curtſey from the performer, who is a king, a queen, or ſome great perſonage, uſually going off the ſtage in diſtreſs, or during the emotions of ſome ſtrong paſſion. If Mr. Garrick, in ſome of his principal characters, was to ſubmit to ſuch a humiliating practice, it would ſurely be at the expence of the audience; who would every inſtant be told, that it was not Lear, Richard, or Macbeth they ſaw before them, but Mr. Garrick.

Friday 13. This morning I viſited the two Signor Bezozzis, whoſe talents are well known to all travellers of taſte in muſic. Their long and uninterrupted regard for each other is as remarkable as their performance. They are brothers; the eldeſt ſeventy, and the youngeſt upwards of ſixty. They have ſo much of the *Idem velle et idem nolle* about them, that they have ever lived together in the utmoſt harmony and affection; carrying their ſimilarity of taſte to their very dreſs, which is the ſame in every particular, even to buttons and buckles. They are batchelors, and have lived ſo long, and in ſo friendly a manner together, that it is thought here, whenever one of them dies, the other will not long ſurvive him. My introduction to theſe eminent performers was eaſy and agreeable, having been favoured with a letter to them from Mr. Giardini, who had been ſo kind as to ſave me the confuſion of aſking them to play upon ſo ſhort an acquaintance, by telling them, in his letter, how much they would oblige me by ſuch a favour. The eldeſt plays the hautbois, and the youngeſt the baſſoon, which inſtrument continues the ſcale of the hautbois, and is its true baſe. Their compoſitions generally conſiſt of ſelect and detached paſſages, yet ſo elaborately finiſhed, that, like ſelect thoughts or maxims in literature, each is not a fragment, but a whole: theſe pieces are in a peculiar manner adapted to diſplay the powers of the performers; but it is difficult

cult to deſcribe their ſtile of playing. Their compoſitions, when printed, give but an imperfect idea of it. So much expreſſion! ſuch delicacy! ſuch a perfect acquieſcence and agreement together, that many of the paſſages ſeem heart-felt ſighs, breathed through the ſame reed. No brilliancy of execution is aimed at, all are notes of meaning. The imitations are exact; the melody is pretty equally diſtributed between the two inſtruments; each *forte*, *piano*, *creſcendo*, *diminuendo*, and *appoggiatura*, is obſerved with a minute exactneſs, which could be attained only by ſuch a long reſidence and ſtudy together. The eldeſt has loſt his under front teeth, and complained of age; and it is natural to ſuppoſe that the performance of each has been better: however, to me, who heard them now for the firſt time, it was charming. If there is any defect in ſo exquiſite a performance, it ariſes from the *equal perfection* of the *two parts*; which diſtracts the attention, and renders it impoſſible to liſten to both, when both have diſſimilar melodies equally pleaſing.

They were born at Parma, and have been upwards of forty years in the ſervice of his Sardinian majeſty, without ever quitting Italy, except in one ſhort excurſion to Paris; or even Turin, but for that journey, and one to viſit the place of their nativity. They are ſober, regular perſons, and are in eaſy circumſtances; have a town and country houſe, in the former are many good pictures, particularly one of Lodovico Carrach, ſuperior to every picture I had ſeen by that maſter.

After this viſit I heard a full piece performed at the king's chapel, and then went to ſee the great opera-houſe, which is reckoned one of the fineſt in Europe. It is very large and elegant; the machinery and decorations are magnificent. I was carried into every part of it, even to the taylor's work-ſhop. Here are ſix rows of boxes above the pit, both larger and deeper

deeper than thoſe of the other theatre: the king is at the chief expence of this opera. Thoſe who have boxes for the ſeaſon, pay, in a kind of fees only, two or three guineas; money at the door being only taken for ſitting in the pit.

The itinerant muſicians, *Anglicè*, ballad-ſingers, and fidlers, at Turin perform in concert. A band of this kind came to the *Hôtel, la bonne femme*, conſiſting of two voices, two violins, a guitar, and baſe, bad enough indeed, though far above our ſcrapers. The ſingers, who were girls, ſung duets very well in tune, accompanied by the whole band. The ſame people at night performed on a ſtage in the *grand place* or ſquare, where they ſold their ballads as our quack doctors do their noſtrums, but with far leſs injury to ſociety. In another part of the ſquare, on a different ſtage, a man and woman ſung Venetian ballads, in two parts, very agreeably, accompanied by a dulcimer.

Saturday 14. Signor Pugnani played a concerto this morning at the king's chapel, which was crowded on the occaſion. It is an elegant rotund, built of black marble, and happily conſtructed for muſic, being very high, and terminated by a dome. I need ſay nothing of the performance of Signor Pugnani, his talents being too well known in England to require it. I ſhall only obſerve, that he did not appear to exert himſelf; and it is not to be wondered at, as neither his Sardinian majeſty, nor any one of the numerous royal family, ſeem to pay much attention to muſic. There is a gloomy ſameneſs at this court, in the daily repetition of ſtate parade and prayer.

Signor Baretti, of this place, in conſequence of a letter from his brother in London, received me very politely, and took great pains to be uſeful to me while I remained in Turin; and in this he ſucceeded very much, by introducing me to

Padre Beccaria, for whom, at firſt ſight, I conceived the higheſt regard and veneration.

He is not above forty; with a large and noble figure, he has ſomething open, natural, intelligent, and benevolent in his countenance, that immediately captivates. We had much converſation concerning electricity, Dr. Franklin, Dr. Prieſtly, and others. He was pleaſed to make me a preſent, finding me an *amateur*, (which ſhould be always tranſlated a *dabler)* of his laſt book *, and the ſyllabus of the *Memoire* he lately ſent to our Royal Society. He likewiſe wrote in my tablets a recommendatory note to M. Laura Baſſi, the famous *dottoreſſa* and academiſt at Bologna; recommended to me ſome books, and was ſo kind, and with a manner ſo truly ſimple, that I ſhall for ever remember this viſit with pleaſure. Mr. Martin,

* *Experimenta, atque Obſervationes, quibus Electricitas vindex late conſtituitur atque explicatur. Taurini:* 1769.

the banker here, came after me to Signor Beccaria's; and this great mathematician is ſo little acquainted with worldly concerns, eſpecially money-matters, that he was quite aſtoniſhed and pleaſed at the ingenuity and novelty of a letter of credit. Mr. Martin deſiring to look at mine, in his preſence, in order to know how he might ſend my letters after me, the good father could hardly comprehend how this letter could be *argent comptant*, ready money, throughout Italy.

He charged me with compliments to *Padre Boſcovich* at Milan, and *Padre Martini* at Bologna; and I left my new acquaintance, impreſſed with the higheſt reſpect and affection for him. I muſt juſt mention one particular more relative to this great and good man, which I had from Signor Baretti; that he, through choice, lives up ſix pair of ſtairs, among his obſervatories, machines, and mathematical inſtruments; and there does every thing for himſelf, even to making his bed, and dreſſing his dinner. I viſit-

I viſited the univerſity, or royal library, where there are fifty thouſand volumes, and many manuſcripts, the catalogue of which fills two volumes in folio. The acceſs to theſe books is eaſy, both before and after dinner, every day, holidays excepted. I was very politely treated there, on Signor Baretti's account, by Signor Grela, the diſtributer of the books, who ſhewed me ſeveral of the moſt ancient MSS.

Among my muſical enquiries at Turin, David Rizio was not forgotten; who having been a native of this city, and his father a muſician here, I thought it likely, if I could find any muſic compoſed by either of them, or by their cotemporaries, that it would determine the long diſputed queſtion, whether David Rizio was author of the Scots melodies attributed to him*.

* The iſſue of this enquiry will be related in the Hiſtory of Muſic.

In my journey from Turin to Milan, I ſtopped a little while at Vercelli; which is a large town, ſaid to contain twenty thouſand inhabitants; where I met with a book on the ſubject of muſic, and with its author, Signor Carlo Geo. Teſtori, with whom I had the pleaſure of converſing.

MILAN.

In this city, which is very large and populous, muſic is much cultivated. Signor Battiſta San Martini is organiſt of two or three churches here; I had a letter to him from Signor Giardini, which procured me a very agreeable reception. He is brother to the famous Martini of London, who ſo long delighted us with his performance on the hautbois, as well as by his compoſitions. The muſic of Signor Battiſta San Martini of Milan is well known in England.

But what I was moſt curious after here, was the Ambroſian Chant or church ſervice,

vice, which is peculiar to Milan, after the manner inſtituted by St. Ambroſe, two hundred years before the Roman, or that of St. Gregory.

At the *Duomo*, or great church, which, in ſize, is ſuperior to every Gothic ſtructure in Italy, and ſaid to be nearly as big as St. Peter's at Rome, there are two large organs, one on each ſide the choir. On feſtivals there are oratorios, *a due cori*, for two choirs, and then both organs are uſed; on common days only one. There are two organiſts; Signor J. Bach, before his arrival in England, was one of them: at preſent the firſt organiſt is Signor G. Corbeli; he is reckoned a very able man in his profeſſion, I heard him play ſeveral times, in a maſterly grave ſtile, ſuited to the place and inſtrument.

Friday, July 17. After hearing the ſervice chanted in the Ambroſian manner, peculiar to this place, I was introduced to Signor Jean Andre Fioroni, *Maeſtro di Capella*

pella at the great church, who invited me into the orcheſtra, ſhewed me the ſervices they were juſt going to ſing, printed on wood, in four parts, the *cantus* and *tenor* on the left ſide, and *altus et baſſus* on the right, without bars. Out of this one book, after the tone was given by the organiſt, the whole four parts were ſung without the organ. There was one boy, and three *caſtrati* for the *ſoprano* and *contr' alto* with two tenors and two baſes, under the direction of Signor Fioroni, who beat the time, and now and then ſung. Theſe ſervices were compoſed about one hundred and fifty years ago, by a Maeſtro di Capella of the *Duomo*, and are much in the ſtile of our ſervices of that time, conſiſting of good harmony, ingenious points and contrivances, but no melody. From hence I went home with Signor Fioroni, who was ſo obliging as to ſhew me all his muſical curioſities, (he had before done me the favour to ſhew me thoſe in the *Sacriſti)* and played over and ſung to

me

me a whole oratorio of his own compoſition. He likewiſe favoured me with a copy of one of his own ſervices, in eight parts in ſcore, for two choirs, which I begged of him, in order to convince the world, that, though the theatrical ſtile and that of the church are now much the ſame, when inſtruments and additional ſingers are employed, yet the ancient grave ſtile is not wholly loſt *.

Piccini had been at Milan this year, during the carnival, for which he compoſed a ſerious opera. The principal ſingers were, firſt man, Signor Aprile; firſt woman, la Signora Piccinelli; and the two principal dancers were M. and Mad. Pique.

After the carnival he compoſed a burletta, called *Il Regno nella Luna*, for the performers, who are ſtill here. Piccini had been gone from hence but a little while before my arrival.

* This piece, with ſeveral other curious compoſitions, mentioned hereafter, will be publiſhed.

There is no ſerious opera at Milan but in carnival time. The firſt burletta I heard there, was *L'Amore Artegiano*; it began at eight, and was not over till twelve o'clock: the muſic, which had pretty things in it, was by Signor Floriano Gaſman, in the ſervice of the emperor, who played the harpſichord. There were in it ſeven characters, all pretty well done, but no one *very* well, as to ſinging.

The dance in this opera was very entertaining; there was an infinite number of principals and figurers employed in it, beſides two *ſaltatori*, Signor and Signora Palecini, who gained more applauſe than all the reſt; indeed their activity was very ſurpriſing: there were two others, who danced *all'Ingleſe*, and there was a French *peruquier* in this burletta, whoſe ſinging was to be French: but their imitations here are ſuch as ours in London, when we are to take off the Italians; that is to ſay, about as like as a miſerable ſign-poſt, called the King or Queen's head, uſually is to George the Third.

Third, or Queen Charlotte: one is more inclined to laugh *at* than *with* ſuch mimics. In this dance the ſtage was illuminated in a moſt ſplendid, and, to me, new manner, with *lampioni coloriti*, or coloured lamps, which had a very pretty effect; the front ſcene and ceiling, as well as the ſides, had an infinite number of theſe lamps.

The theatre here is very large and ſplendid; it has five rows of boxes on each ſide, one hundred in each row; and parallel to theſe runs a broad gallery, round the houſe, as an avenue to every row of boxes: each box will contain ſix perſons, who ſit at the ſides, facing each other. Acroſs the gallery of communication is a complete room to every box, with a fireplace in it, and all conveniences for refreſhments and cards. In the fourth row is a *pharo* table, on each ſide the houſe, which is uſed during the performance of the opera. There is in front a very large box, as big as a common London dining-room, ſet apart for the Duke of Modena, governor of Milan, and the *Principeſſina* his daughter, who were both there. The noiſe here during the performance was abominable, except while two or three airs and a duet were ſinging, with which every one was in raptures : at the end of the duet, the applauſe continued with unremitting violence till the performers returned to ſing it again, which is here the way of encoring a favourite air. The firſt violin was played by Lucchini : the band is very numerous, and orcheſtra large in proportion to the ſize of the theatre, which is much bigger than the great opera-houſe at Turin. In the higheſt ſtory the people ſit in front; and thoſe for whom there are no ſeats, ſtand behind in the gallery: all the boxes here are appropriated for the ſeaſon, as at Turin. Between the acts the company from the pit come up ſtairs, and walk about the galleries. There was only one dance, but that very long.

It is not the Engliſh genius to be ſatisfied with their preſent condition or poſſeſſions, or elſe, upon the whole, one may venture to pronounce, that ſuch a comic opera as that of laſt winter in London, might have contented them; which, on the ſide of ſinging, was greatly ſuperior to this; nor did I meet, throughout Italy, with three ſuch performers at leaſt on the ſame ſtage, as Signor Lovatini, Signor Morigi, and Signora Guadagni.

The opera here is carried on by thirty noblemen, who ſubſcribe ſixty zechins each, for which every ſubſcriber has a box*; the reſt of the boxes are let for the year at fifty zechins *la prima fila*, or firſt row, forty the ſecond, thirty the third, and in proportion for the reſt. The chance money only ariſes from the pit and upper ſeats, or *picconai:* they perform every night except Fridays.

* A zechin is a gold coin, current all over Italy, equal in value to about nine ſhillings Engliſh.

Wednesday 18. I went this morning, for the firſt time, to the Ambroſian Library, which, in ſize, appears but diminutive, after reading the accounts given of it in books of travels, and after having ſeen the *Bibliotèque du Roi* at Paris, which is, at leaſt, ten times as big; there is, in fact, but one large room filled with printed books, and two ſmall ones for French literature, printed and MS. then a room full of copies only of the beſt ancient ſtatues at Rome and Florence; and, laſtly, a large hall or ſaloon, full indeed of wonderful performances of the greateſt painters; among theſe are many ineſtimable works of Leonardo da Vinci, and Jean Breugel, of Antwerp, the high finiſher, whoſe four elements in this collection are ſaid to have coſt him his ſight. There is an admirable portrait in the collection, by this painter, of the organiſt Merula *. Upon

* Claudius Merulus, as the Germans called him, was of Antwerp, and flouriſhed in the ſixteenth century.

my

my enquiring for the catalogue of MSS. I was told it was not ufual to fhew it, but I might fee any one in the collection, if I would afk for it by name; but I knew no more the name than the contents: I was in queft of new exiftences, new literary beings, unpolluted by profane compilers and printers. Upon explaining my errand to Milan, and faying it was chiefly to afcertain the time of eftablifhing the Ambrofian Chant in that church, I was told that *Padre Martini* had made the fame enquiries, but without fuccefs; it feeming as if that chant had been given to St. Ambrofe by the writers of his life, one after the other, without fufficient proof. This was rather difcouraging; however I did not, as yet, give up the point; and I afterwards found more favour in the fight of the librarians. As yet I had not delivered my letters to thofe perfons, whofe countenance, in my future vifits, procured me every fatisfaction this library could afford.

A gentleman of Parma, with whom I had travelled from Paris, having a letter from M. Meſſier to Padre Boſcovich, giving him an account of a new comet which he had diſcovered on the eleventh of June, I had the pleaſure of accompanying my friend in his viſit to this father at the Jeſuits College, who received us both with great courteſy; and being told that I was an Engliſhman, a lover of the ſciences, and ambitious of ſeeing ſo celebrated a man, he addreſſed himſelf to me in a particular manner. He had ſeveral young ſtudents of quality with him, and ſaid he expected that morning three perſons of diſtinction to ſee his inſtruments, and invited me to be of the party; I gladly accepted the propoſal, and he immediately began to ſhew and explain to me ſeveral machines and contrivances which he had invented for making optical experiments, before the arrival of the *Signori*, who were a Knight of Malta, a nephew of Pope Benedict XIV. and another

another *Cavaliere*. He then went on, and ſurpriſed and delighted us all very much, particularly with his *Stet Sol*, by which he can fix the ſun's rays, paſſing through an aperture or a priſm, to any part of the oppoſite wall he pleaſes: he likewiſe ſeparates and fixes any of the priſmatic colours of the rays. Shewed us a method of forming an aquatic priſm, and the effects of joining different lenſes, all extremely plain and ingenious. He has publiſhed a Latin diſſertation on theſe matters at Vienna. Then we aſcended to different obſervatories, where I found his inſtruments mounted in ſo ingenious and ſo convenient a manner, as to give me the utmoſt pleaſure. He was ſo polite as to addreſs himſelf to me always in French, as I had at firſt accoſted him in that language, and in which I was at this time much more at my eaſe than in Italian. M. Meſſier had told him the comet had very little motion, being almoſt ſtationary; but Padre Boſcovich afterwards found it ſo rapid as to move fifty degrees in a day. *Mais la comete, Monſieur, lui dis-je, ou eſt elle a preſent? Avec le ſoleil, elle eſt mariée.* The late Duke of York made him a preſent of one of Short's twelve-inch reflectors, of twenty guineas price; but he has an acromatic one, by the ſame maker, which coſt one hundred. The expence of his obſervatory, which is defrayed by himſelf, muſt have been enormous. He is univerſity profeſſor at Pavia, where he ſpends his winters. If any new diſcoveries are to be made in aſtronomy, they may be expected from this learned Jeſuit; whoſe attention to optical experiments for the improvement of glaſſes, upon which ſo much depends; and whoſe great number of admirable inſtruments of all ſorts, joined to the excellence of the climate, and the wonderful ſagacity he has diſcovered in the conſtruction of his obſervatory and machines, form a concurrence of favourable circumſtances, not eaſily

eaſily to be found elſewhere. He complained very much of the ſilence of the Engliſh aſtronomers, who anſwer none of his letters. He was ſeven months in England, and during that time was very much with Mr. Maſkaline, Dr. Shepherd, Dr. Bevis, and Dr. Maty, with whom he hoped to keep up a correſpondence. He had, indeed, lately received from Mr. Profeſſor Maſkaline the laſt Nautical Almanack, with Mayer's Lunar Tables, who gave him hopes of reviving their literary intercourſe. He is a tall, ſtrong built man, upwards of fifty, of a very agreeable addreſs. He was refuſed admiſſion into the French academy, when at Paris, though a member, by the parliament, on account of his being a Jeſuit: but if all Jeſuits were like this father, making uſe only of ſuperior learning and intellects for the advancement of ſcience, and the happineſs of mankind, one would have wiſhed this ſociety to be as durable as the world. As it is, it ſeems as if equity

equity required that ſome diſcrimination ſhould be made in condemning the Jeſuits; for though good policy may require a diſſolution of their order, yet humanity certainly makes one wiſh to preſerve the old, the infirm, and the innocent, from the general wreck and deſtruction due only to the guilty.

The ſecond opera I heard here was *La Lavandara Aſtuta*, a *Paſticcio*, with a large portion of Piccini's airs in it. Garibaldi, the firſt man, had a better part in this burletta than in the firſt, and ſung very well. He has a pleaſing voice, and much taſte and expreſſion; was encored, *alla Italiana*, two or three times. One of the *Baglioni* * ſings better than the two others, and had more to do. Caratoli diverted the people at Milan very much by his action and humour, though local, and what would not pleaſe in England: the

* There are ſix ſiſters of that name, all ſingers, three of them were at Milan: 'tis a Bologneſe family.

dance

dance was the ſame as that I had ſeen before.

A private concert in Italy is called an *accademia*; the firſt I went to was compoſed entirely of *dilettanti*; *il padrone*, or the maſter of the houſe, played the firſt violin, and had a very powerful hand; there were twelve or fourteen performers, among whom were ſeveral good violins; there were likewiſe two German flutes, a violoncello, and ſmall double baſe; they executed, reaſonably well, ſeveral of our Bach's ſymphonies, different from thoſe printed in England: all the muſic here is in MS. But what I liked moſt was the vocal part by *La Signora Padrona della Caſa*, or lady of the houſe; ſhe had an agreeable well-toned voice, a good ſhake, the right ſort of taſte and expreſſion, and ſung (ſitting down, with the paper on the common inſtrumental deſk) wholly without affectation, ſeveral pretty airs of Traetta.

Upon

Upon the whole, this concert was much upon a level with our own private concerts among gentlemen in England, the performers were ſometimes in and ſometimes out; in general, however, the muſic was rather better choſen, the execution more brilliant and full of fire, and the ſinging much nearer perfection than we can often boaſt on ſuch occaſions; not, indeed, in point of voice or execution, for in reſpect to them our females are, at leaſt, equal to our neighbours, but in the *portamento* or direction of the voice, in expreſſion and in diſcretion *.

* It is humbly hoped that my fair countrywomen will not take offence at the uſe of the word *diſcretion*, as its acceptation here is wholly confined to muſic, in which the love for what is commonly called *gracing*, is carried to ſuch a pitch of *indiſcretion*, as frequently to change paſſages from good to bad, and from bad to worſe. A *little* paint may embelliſh an ordinary face, though a great deal would render it hideous; but true beauty is ſurely beſt in its natural ſtate.

The ſame day, Friday, July 20, there was muſic at three different churches; I wiſhed to be at them all during the performances, but it was impoſſible to be preſent at more than two of them; the firſt of which was in the morning, at the church of *Santa Maria Secreta*; it was a *Meſſa in muſica*, by Signor Monza, and under his direction: his brother played the principal violoncello, with much facility of execution, but neither in tone or taſte very pleaſing. The firſt violin was played by Signor Lucchini, who leads at the burletta; there were two or three *caſtrati* among the ſingers. A little paltry organ was erected on the occaſion; there was a large one in the church, but it ſtood in a gallery, which was too ſmall for a band: the muſic was pretty; long and ingenious introductory ſymphonies to each *concento*, as each part or diviſion of the maſs is called; and the whole was in good taſte, and ſpirited; but the organ, hautbois, and ſome of the fiddles being bad, deſtroyed the effect of ſeveral things that were well deſigned. As a principal violin, Signor Lucchini is not of the firſt claſs; there is no want of hand, but great want of finiſhing: he had ſeveral ſolo parts given him, and made three or four cloſes.

The ſinging, though in general rather better than at our oratorios, was by no means ſo good as we often hear in England at the Italian opera. As yet I had met with no *great* ſinger ſince my arrival in Italy. The firſt *ſoprano* here was what we ſhould call in England a pretty good ſinger, with a pretty good voice; his taſte neither original nor ſuperior. The ſecond ſinger, a *contr' alto*, had likewiſe but a moderate portion of merit; though his voice was pleaſing, and he never gave offence by the injudicious uſe of it. But,

> "'Tis in *ſong* as it 'tis in painting,
> Much may be right, yet much be wanting."

However, ſuch a performance as this ſhould not be criticiſed too ſeverely, for

it

it is heard for nothing. I ſpeak as a traveller; but the people of Italy, who contribute ſo much to the ſupport of the church, are ſurely well entitled to have theſe treats excellent.

The ſecond maſs I heard to-day was compoſed by Battiſta San Martini, and performed under his direction at the church of the Carmini; the ſymphonies were very ingenious, and full of the ſpirit and fire peculiar to that author. The inſtrumental parts in his compoſitions are well written; he lets none of the performers be long idle; and the violins, eſpecially, are never ſuffered to ſleep. It might, however, ſometimes be wiſhed that he would ride his *Pegaſus* with a curb-bridle; for he ſeems abſolutely to run away with him. Without metaphor, his muſic would pleaſe more if there were fewer notes, and fewer *allegros* in it: but the impetuoſity of his genius impels him to run on in a ſucceſſion of rapid movements, which in the end fatigue both the performer and the hearers. Marchesini, whom I did not much like, sung the first *soprano* part; Ciprandi, an excellent tenor, who was in England a few years ago, and whose cast of parts has never since been so well filled, sung here in a manner far superior to all the rest. The band was but indifferent; the first violin was played by Zuccherini, who is reckoned here a good musician. I find performances of this kind but ill attended, no people of fashion are ever seen at them; the congregation seems to consist principally of the clergy, trades-people, mechanics, country clowns, and beggars, who are, for the most part, very inattentive and restless, seldom remaining in the church during the whole performance. San Martini is *Maestro di Capella* to half the churches in Milan, and the number of masses he has composed is almost infinite; however his fire and invention still remain in their utmost vigour.

At another church veſpers were performed this evening by Monks and Nuns only; I was too late in my attempt to hear them: however I was carried to one of the largeſt *accademia* of Milan, where there were upwards of thirty performers, and among them ſeveral good ones. Madame Dé ſung; and though ſhe had a cold, which affected her voice, did ſeveral things which diſcovered her to have the abilities of a capital ſinger. Beſides two ſongs of great compaſs and execution, ſhe ſung an *adagio* with infinite taſte. The maſter at the harpſichord was Signor Scotti; two or three of Mr. Bach's overtures were played, and very much approved; and an excellent one of Martini, with a duet violin concerto of Raymond, a German, very well written, and, though difficult, well performed, by two violins of different powers, but both good in their way; one an elderly man, with great neatneſs and delicacy of tone, but feeble; the other very young, with a force and fire which will ſoon render him a very great player; eſpecially as to theſe requiſites he joins expreſſion: it was an admirable conteſt between age and youth, judgment and genius. Theſe were all *virtuoſi* or profeſſors, the reſt of the band was made up of *dilettanti.*

Saturday 21. It did not ſeem foreign to my buſineſs in Italy to viſit the *Palazzo Simonetto,* a mile or two from Milan, to hear the famous echo, about which travellers have ſaid ſo much, that I rather ſuſpected exaggeration. This is not the place to enter deeply into the doctrine of reverberation; I ſhall reſerve the attempt for another work; as to the matter of fact, this echo is very wonderful. The *Simonetto* palace is near no other building; the country all around is a dead flat, and no mountains are nearer than thoſe of Swiſſerland, which are upwards of thirty miles off. This palace is now uninhabited and in ruin, but has been pretty; the front is open, and ſupported by very

light

light double Ionic pillars, but the echo is only to be heard behind the houſe, which, next to the garden has two wings.

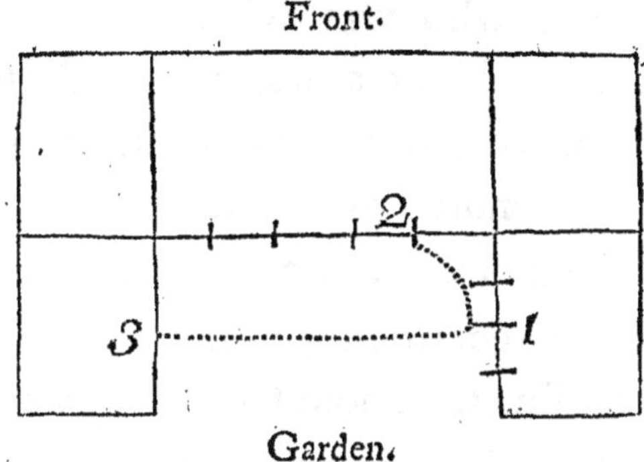

1. The beſt window to make the experiment at.

2. The beſt window to hear the echo from.

3. A dead wall with only windows painted upon it, from whence the repetitions ſeem to proceed.

Now, though it is natural to ſuppoſe that the oppoſite walls reflect the ſound, it is not eaſy to ſay in what manner; as the form of the building is a very common one, and no other of the ſame construc-

 tion,

tion, that I have ever heard of, produces the ſame effects. I made experiments of all kinds, and in every ſituation, with the voice, ſlow, quick; with a trumpet, which a ſervant who was with me ſounded; with a piſtol, and a muſquet, and always found agreeable to the doctrine of echos, that the more quick and violent the percuſſion of the air, the more numerous were the repetitions; which, upon firing the muſquet, amounted to upwards of fifty, of which the ſtrength ſeemed regularly to diminiſh, and the diſtance to become more remote. Such a muſical canon might be contrived for one fine voice here, according to father Kircher's method, as would have all the effect of two, three, and even four voices. One blow of a hammer produced a very good imitation of an ingenious and practiſed footman's knock at a London door, on a viſiting night. A ſingle *ha!* became a long horſe-laugh; and a forced note, or a ſound overblown in the trumpet, became the

the moſt ridiculous and laughable noiſe imaginable.

The compoſers to be found in this city are innumerable. I was carried to-day to hear three ladies ſing, who are ſiſters, and I found at their houſe Signor Lampugnani, who is their maſter: he lives conſtantly at Milan, plays the firſt harpſichord at the opera, in the abſence of the compoſers, and puts together the *paſticcios*. Theſe ladies did him great credit, by the manner in which they ſung ſeveral ſongs, duets, and trios. One of them performed a long ſcene in the *Olimpiade* of Jomelli, which is extremely difficult; the compoſition is juſtly admired for the boldneſs and learning in the modulation, which is *recherchée*, but expreſſive and pleaſing: I have procured a copy of this ſcene. There was at the ſame houſe a good performer on the violin, Signor Paſqualini, who accompanied the ſongs with great neatneſs and judgment.

After this I went to the opera-houſe, where the audience was very much diſappointed; the firſt tenor, and only good ſinger in it, being ill. All his part was cut out, and the *Baritono*, in the character of a bluſtering old father, who was to abuſe his ſon violently in the firſt ſcene and ſong, finding he had no ſon there, gave a turn to the misfortune, which diverted the audience very much, and made them ſubmit to their diſappointment with a better grace than they would have done in England; for inſtead of his ſon, he fell foul on the prompter, who here, as at the opera in England, pops his head out of a little trap-door on the ſtage. The audience were ſo delighted with this attack upon the prompter, who is ever regarded as an enemy to their pleaſures, that they encored the ſong in which it was made. However, after the firſt act and the dance, I came away, as the lights at the opera-houſe here affected my eyes in a very painful manner; and there being

no

no retribution for this ſuffering to-night, I denied myſelf the reſt of the performance.

Sunday 22. This morning, after hearing the Ambroſian ſervice in all its perfection, at the *Duomo,* I went to the Convent of *Santa Maria Maddalena*; I heard ſeveral motets performed by the nuns; it was their feaſt-day. The compoſition was by Signor B. S. Martini, who is *Maeſtro di Capella*, and teaches to ſing at this convent. He made me ample amends for the want of ſlow movements in his maſs on Friday, by an *adagio* in the motet of to-day, which was truly divine, and divinely ſung by one of the ſiſters, accompanied, on the organ only, by another. It was by far the beſt ſinging, in every reſpect, I had heard ſince my arrival in Italy; where there is ſo much, that one ſoon grows faſtidious. At my firſt coming I both hungered and thirſted after muſic, but I now had had almoſt my fill; and we are more ſevere critics upon a full ſtomach, than with a good appetite. Several of the nuns ſung, ſome but indifferently, but one of them had an excellent voice; full, rich, ſweet, and flexible, with a true ſhake, and exquiſite expreſſion; it was delightful, and left nothing to wiſh, but duration!

There is a general complaint in England againſt loud accompaniments; and if an evil there, it is doubly ſuch in Italy. In the opera-houſe nothing but the inſtruments can be heard, unleſs when the *baritoni* or baſe voices ſing, who can contend with them; nothing but noiſe can be heard through noiſe; a delicate voice is ſuffocated: it ſeems to me as if the orcheſtra not only played too loud, but had too much to do.

Beſides the organ in this convent for the choruſſes, there was an organ and harpſichord together, which was likewiſe played by one of the nuns; and the accompaniment of that inſtrument alone with

with the heavenly voice abovementioned, pleafed me beyond defcription, and not fo much by what it *did*, as by what it did *not* do; furely one cannot hear too much of fuch a mellifluous voice. All the jargon of different parts, of laboured contrivance, and difficult execution, is little better than an ugly mafk upon a beautiful face; even harmony itfelf, upon fuch occafions is an evil, when it becomes a fovereign inftead of a fubject. I know this is not fpeaking like a *mufician*, but I fhall always give up the *profeffion*, when it inclines to pedantry; and give way to my feelings, when they feem to have reafon on their fide. If a voice be coarfe, or otherwife difpleafing, the lefs it is heard the better, and then tumultuous accompaniments and artful contrivances may have their ufe; but a fingle note from fuch a voice as that I heard this morning, penetrates deeper into the foul, than the fame note from the moft perfect inftrument upon earth can do, which,

at

at beſt, is but an imitation of the human voice.

The muſic this morning was entirely performed by the nuns themſelves, who were inviſible to the congregation; and though the church of the convent is open to the public, like a common pariſh church, in which the prieſts are in ſight, as elſewhere, yet the reſponſes are made behind the altar, where the organ is placed. I looked in vain for that and the ſingers, upon my firſt entrance into the church, without knowing it belonged to a convent. Upon my praiſing this ſinging, I was told that there were ſeveral convents here in which the nuns ſing much better. Of this I muſt own I was in doubt; I could only ſay I ſhould be very glad to hear them. And I was ſo pleaſed with this ſinging, that though I dined with a private family, in a very ſociable and agreeable way, I ran from the company ere the ſecond courſe was ſerved, in hopes of hearing more of it at the

the ſame convent; and was ſo fortunate as to enter it juſt as the ſervice was begun, and heard the ſame motet repeated again by the ſame nun, and with double delight.

The ballad-ſingers at Milan ſing duets in the ſtreets, ſometimes with, and ſometimes without inſtruments, and keep very firm to their parts; but I did not perceive that they mount a ſtage here as at Turin.

At night, the firſt tenor of the burletta continuing to be ill, there was an *accademia* at the theatre, inſtead of an opera. The ſingers were the ſame that I had heard before; they were placed on the ſtage in much the ſame manner as at the annual performance in London for the benefit of decayed muſicians: they ſat at tables, two and two, and when they ſung, each got up, and advanced towards the audience. There were ſeveral opera overtures performed, but no ſolos; inſtead of them there were dances between the

acts

acts of the concert. On the ſtage, behind the ſingers, which were ſix, there ſtood ſix ſervants the whole time. The *Baglioni* appeared to more advantage to-night than in the opera, eſpecially Clementina, who, in a leſs theatre, would be a very agreeable ſinger; in this all voices are loſt.

Monday 23. This morning I went early with father Moiana, a very agreeable Dominican, to the Ambroſian Library, and with ſome difficulty got a ſight of two or three very ancient manuſcripts relative to my purpoſe, and of the pompous edition of the ſervices performed at the Duomo, printed in four vaſt volumes in folio, 1619, for the uſe of that church only. The printing is very neat, upon wood, but without bars, and conſequently not in ſcore, though the parts are all in ſight, upon oppoſite pages; *ſoprano* and *tenor* on the firſt, and *alto* and *baſſo* on the ſecond page: I made ſeveral extracts from

from all theſe. Signor Oltrocchi, the librarian, began to be more communicative than at firſt. One of the moſt ancient books he ſhewed me this morning, was a beautiful manuſcript of the ninth century, and well preſerved. It is a miſſal, written before the time of Guido, at leaſt two hundred years, and conſequently before the lines uſed by that monk were invented. The notes are little more than accents of different kinds put over the hymns *. I met with a noble and learned churchman here, Don Triulzi, a perſon very much in years, who had ſtudied theſe characters, and had formed ſome ingenious conjectures about them.

The reſt of this day was ſpent in queſt of old books, and the evening in hearing muſic. Chieſa and Monza ſeem, and are ſaid to be the two beſt compoſers for the ſtage here at preſent. Serbelloni, a *contr'alto caſtrato*, who was in England ſome

* A ſpecimen of this notation will be given in the General Hiſtory of Muſic.

years ago, has had a diſpenſation to become a prieſt, and now only ſings in the church.

Tueſday 24. This morning a ſolemn proceſſion paſſed through the ſtreets to the church of St. Ambroſe for rain, on which account the public library was not open, which was a great diſappointment to me, being the laſt day I had to ſtay here; but by this time my letters had procured me the notice and countenance of his Excellency *Count Fermian,* the *Conte Pò, il Marcheſe Menaſoglio, D. Franceſco Carcano,* the *Abate Bonelli,* and others; which operated like *magic* in opening doors and removing difficulties; and upon my preſenting myſelf at the Ambroſian Library with the *Abate Bonelli,* it was inſtantly opened; and, indeed, for the firſt time, all its treaſures; the moſt curious MSS. were now diſplayed; among which were ſeveral books of Petrarca's and Leonardo da Vinci's own hand-writing. I was likewiſe ſhewn ſeveral very ancient MSS. upon *papyrus*, well preſerved. In ſhort, I was made ample amends this morning for former diſappointments, being carried into a room containing nothing but MSS. to the amount of fifteen thouſand volumes.

From hence the *Abate* carried me to *Padre Sacchi*, a learned muſician here, as to theory; he has publiſhed two very curious books, relative to muſic, which I had before purchaſed. He received me very courteouſly, and we entered deeply into converſation on the ſubject of them and of my journey. He was ſo obliging as to write down my direction, and gave me great encouragement to write to him, if on reading his books I met with any difficulties.

BRESCIA.

Thurſday, July 26. I was only one day in this town, but, it happening to be a holiday, I had the good fortune to hear a boy, at the church of the Jeſuits *delle*

Grazie,

Grazie, whose voice and volubility pleased me much. His name is Carlo Moschetti, a scholar of Pietro Pellegrino, *Maestra di Capella* of this church, who beat the time during the performance of his motet. This *castrato* is not above fourteen or fifteen. He has a compass of two octaves complete, from the middle C in the scale to the highest. His voice is full, when he has time to throw it out; and he executes swift passages with such facility, that he is apt to be lavish and run riot, and now and then is not exactly in tune. But there seems to be good stuff for a master to work upon; his shake is good, and he promises to be a great singer. There was a young counter tenor, of whom little is to be said; a tenor, less; and a base that drove me out of the church.

At a kind of Magdalen Hospital in this place, the women were singing and playing most furiously; the music was in the old stile, full of fugues upon hackneyed

subjects

ſubjects. Theſe females do the whole buſineſs, upon ſuch occaſions, themſelves; play the organ, violins, and baſes: the performance indeed was ſo coarſe, that I had ſoon enough of it. I heard no organs in this town that ſeemed to be well toned, but then they are much ornamented, and, like the French opera, more calculated to pleaſe the eye than the ear. The pipes here are never gilt, though ſometimes the frame and caſe are, and have not a bad effect.

The theatre at Breſcia is very ſplendid, but it is much leſs than that at Milan, with reſpect to length; the height is the ſame. The proportion of boxes round each theatre is as one hundred to thirty-four: there are five rows in each, ſo that this houſe ſeems much higher than that at Milan. The boxes are more ornamented with glaſſes, paintings, front-cloths of velvet, or rich ſilks fringed; more room is allowed here in the pit, to each auditor, than at Milan; every ſeat turns up, and is locked till the person comes who has taken it; and here every row, and every box of each row, is numbered, as in our playhouses, when the pit and boxes are laid together. The comedy was *Il Saggio Amico*, the Prudent Friend, written by Goldoni; it was the first I had ever seen in Italy without a Harlequin, Colombine, Pierro, and Dottore: it was more like a regular comedy than the Italian pieces usually are. There was a *Milordo Inglese* in it, who gave away his zechins by handfuls, with which the audience was very much pleased. Some of the actors came on with candles in their hands; it never struck me before, but, on the English and French stage, where this is not practised, probability suffers when the transactions of the piece are supposed to happen in the night.

Here was a burletta in run, under the direction of Signor Leopoldo Maria Scherli, *Maestro di Capella*; the singers were Giovanni Simoni, Giuseppe Franceschini,

ceſchini, Niccola Menichelli, Angiola Dotti, Geltrude Dotti, Tereſa Menichelli, Tereſa Monti, but, for my misfortune, they did not perform while I was at Breſcia.

At the ſign of the *Gambero* or Lobſter, where I lodged, and in the next room to mine, there was a company of opera ſingers, who ſeemed all very jolly; they were juſt come from Ruſſia, where they had been fourteen or fifteen years. The principal ſinger among them, I found, upon enquiry, to be the *Caſtrato* Luini Bonetto. He is ſaid to be ſtill very rich, though he loſt in one night, at play, ten thouſand pounds of the money he had gained *per la ſua virtù*. He is a native of Breſcia; was welcomed home by a band of muſic, at the inn, the night of his arrival, and by another the night before his and my departure, conſiſting of two violins, a mandoline, French horn, trumpet, and violoncello; and, though in the dark, they played long concertos, with ſolo parts for the mandoline. I was ſurpriſed at the memory of theſe performers; in ſhort, it was excellent *ſtreet* muſic, and ſuch as we are not accuſtomed to; but ours is not a climate for ſerenades. The famous Venetian dancer, La Colonna, was likewiſe juſt arrived from Ruſſia, and in the ſame houſe; they were all going to Venice.

VERONA.

There was no opera in this city, ſerious or comic, when I arrived in it, July 28; however, I was conducted to the famous amphitheatre, ſaid to have been built by Auguſtus, or, at leaſt, about his time; perhaps by Vitruvius, who was not only his architect, but a native of Verona. The inſide has been lately repaired, and is entire: it has forty-ſix rows of ſeats, of rough white marble; is of an oval figure, the greateſt diameter being two hundred and thirty-three feet, and

and leaſt one hundred and thirty-ſix: the inhabitants ſay that it will contain ſixty thouſand perſons, which is more than twice the number at preſent in Verona. It was here that the people were formerly amuſed with wild beaſts, and upon my entrance into it, I really thought it had been ſtill appropriated to that purpoſe, for the roaring and noiſe which aſſailed my ears, ſeemed to proceed from nothing human; when, behold, upon a nearer approach I found it was only *Pantalone* and *Brighello*, who had been baited and beaten by Harlequin; indeed this gentleman's wit had great force to-night, and, I believe, contributed more to the happineſs of the ſpectators, than ever the elephants, lions, or tigers did in former times. The comedy, in which theſe characters were introduced, was repreſented in all its buffoon perfection; and I now ſaw, for the firſt time, *Harlequin*, *Brighello*, *Pantalone*, and *Colombina*, in true Italian purity. The ſtage was erected in the middle of the *arena*; there were only two boxes, one on each ſide the ſtage: the area before the ſtage made a kind of pit, where the better ſort of company ſat on chairs. The next beſt places were on the ſteps, about twelve deep, railed off from the reſt of the ſteps, which may be regarded as the upper gallery; but all this in the open air, and the ſeats the naked marble. Here is a modern theatre, but that is only uſed in the winter for the opera *.

VICENZA.

There was neither opera nor comedy at this place when I paſſed through it, nor ſhould I have mentioned this city in

* The ſhort ſpace of time I ſtaid at Verona, was not ſufficient for many muſical enquiries; but I was afterwards informed by an Engliſh gentleman, who had reſided ſeveral years in that city, that it contains, beſides ſeveral able profeſſors, a great number of *dilettanti*, who both perform and compoſe in a ſuperior manner.

my

my journal, had I not been entertained, during dinner, with a kind of vocal muſic which I had not before heard in Italy: it conſiſted of a pſalm, in three parts, performed by boys of different ages, who were proceeding from their ſchool to the cathedral, in proceſſion, with their maſter, a prieſt, at their head, who ſung the baſe. There was more melody than uſual in this kind of muſic; and though they marched through the ſtreet very faſt, yet they ſung very well in time and tune. Theſe boys are a kind of religious *preſs-gang*, who ſeize all other boys they can find in their way to the church, in order to be catechiſed.

In coming from Verona to this city, I overtook a great number of pilgrims, young men, who were going to Venice to viſit the tomb of St. Francis; they uſed to go to Loretto once a year, but the ſenate has forbidden them to go out of the Venetian territories. Several of them marched in large companies, and ſung, or rather chanted, hymns and psalms in *canto fermo*.

PADUA.

This city has been rendered no less famous, of late years, by the residence of Tartini, the celebrated composer and performer on the violin, than in ancient times, by having given birth to the great historian Livy. But Tartini died a few months before my arrival here, an event which I regarded as a particular misfortune to myself, as well as a loss to the whole musical world; for he was a professor, whom I was not more desirous to hear perform, than ambitious to converse with. I visited the street and house where he had lived; the church and grave where he was buried; his bust, his successor, his executor, and every thing, however minute and trivial, which could afford me the least intelligence concerning his life and character, with the zeal of a pilgrim at Mecca: and though, since his death,

all

all theſe particulars are become hiſtorical, and hardly belong to the *preſent ſtate* of muſic; yet I ſhould be inclined to preſent the reader with a ſketch of his life, if my books and papers collected in the Venetian ſtate, among which are the materials I acquired at Padua concerning Tartini, were arrived. As it is, I ſhall only ſay, that he was born at Pirano, in Iſtria, in 1692; that, in his early youth, having manifeſted an attachment to a young perſon, who was regarded as unworthy of being allied to his family, his father ſhut him up; and during his confinement he amuſed himſelf with muſical inſtruments, in order to divert his melancholy; ſo that it was by mere accident he diſcovered in himſelf the ſeeds of thoſe talents which afterwards grew into ſo much eminence.

M. de la Lande ſays he had from his own mouth the following ſingular anecdote, which ſhews to what degree his imagination was inflamed by the genius of of compoſition. "He dreamed one "night, in 1713, that he had made a "compact with the Devil, who promiſed "to be at his ſervice on all occaſions; "and during this viſion every thing "ſucceeded according to his mind; his "wiſhes were prevented, and his deſires "always ſurpaſſed by the aſſiſtance of "his new ſervant. In ſhort, he imagined "he gave the Devil his violin, in order "to diſcover what kind of a muſician he "was; when, to his great aſtoniſhment, "he heard him play a ſolo ſo ſingularly "beautiful, and executed with ſuch ſu-"perior taſte and preciſion, that it ſur-"paſſed all he had ever heard or con-"ceived in his life. So great was his "ſurpriſe, and ſo exquiſite his delight "upon this occaſion, that it deprived "him of the power of breathing. He "awoke with the violence of this ſenſa-"tion, and inſtantly ſeized his fiddle, in "hopes of expreſſing what he had juſt "heard, but in vain; he, however, then

"com-

"composed a piece, which is perhaps, "the best of all his works, (he called it "the Devil's Sonata) but it was so in- "ferior to what his sleep had produced, "that he declared he should have broken "his instrument, and abandoned music "for ever, if he could have subsisted by "any other means." *

He married early a wife of the Xantippe sort, and his patience upon the most trying occasions was always truly Socratic. He had no other children than his scholars, of whom his care was constantly paternal. Nardini, his first, and favourite pupil, came from Leghorn to see him in his sickness, and attend him in his last moments, with true filial affection and tenderness. During the latter part of his life he played but little, except at the church of St. Anthony of Padua, to which he had devoted himself so early as the year 1722, where, though he had a salary of four hundred ducats a year, yet his attendance was only required on great festi-

* *Voyage d'un François.* Tom. 8.

festivals; but so strong was his zeal for the service of his patron saint, that he seldom let a week pass without regaling him to the utmost power of his palsied nerves.

He died universally regretted by the Patavinians, who had long been amused by his talents, and edified by his piety and good works. To his Excellency Count *Torre Taxis* of Venice, his scholar and protector, he bequeathed his MS. music; and to the professor *Padre Colombo*, who had long been his friend and counsellor, he left the care of a posthumous work, of which, though chiefly mathematical, the theory of sound makes a considerable part *.

There was a public function performed for him at Padua, March 31, 1770, at which a funeral oration was pronounced by the *Abate Francesco Fanzago*, and an anthem performed, which was composed

* In this work he proposed to remove the obscurity, and explain the difficulties of which he is accused in his former Treatises.

on

on the occaſion by Signor P. Maeſtro Valloti.

His merit, both as a compoſer and performer, is too well known to need a panegyric here: I ſhall only ſay, that as a compoſer, he was one of the few original geniuſſes of this age, who conſtantly drew from his own ſource; that his melody was full of fire and fancy, and his harmony, though learned, yet ſimple and pure; and as a performer, that his ſlow movements evince his taſte and expreſſion, and his lively ones his great hand. He was the firſt who knew and taught the power of the bow; and his knowledge of the finger-board is proved by a thouſand beautiful paſſages, to which that alone could give birth. His ſcholar, Nardini, who played to me many of his beſt ſolos, as I thought, very well, with reſpect to correctneſs and expreſſion, aſſured me that his dear and honoured maſter, as he conſtantly called him, was as much ſuperior to himſelf, in the performance

formance of the ſame ſolos, both in the pathetic and brilliant parts, as he was to any one of his ſcholars.

With regard to the complaint made by common readers, of obſcurity in his Treatiſe of Muſic, and the abuſe of mathematics, of which he is accuſed by men of ſcience, they are points which this is not the place to diſcuſs. Perhaps a more exact character of this work cannot be given than that of M. Rouſſeau, who ſays, "If the Syſtem of the celebrated Tartini is not that of nature, it is at leaſt "that of which the principles are the moſt "ſimple, and from which all the laws "of harmony ſeem to ariſe in a leſs arbitrary manner, than in any other "which has been hitherto publiſhed *." That his Syſtem is full of new and ingenious ideas, which could only ariſe

* Since this Journal was prepared for the preſs, a book has been publiſhed under the title of *Principles and Power of Harmony*; from which I have received the higheſt pleaſure that an elegant, clear, and maſterly performance can give. Who the author

from a ſuperior knowledge in his art, may be diſcovered through its veil of obſcurity; and his friend *Padre Colombo* accounted to me for that obſcurity and appearance of want of true ſcience, by confeſſing that Tartini, with all the parade of figures, and ſolutions of problems, was no mathematician, and that he did not underſtand common arithmetic well. However, he ſaw more than he could expreſs by terms or principles borrowed from any other ſcience; and though neither a geometrician or an algebraiſt, he had a facility and method of calculating peculiar to himſelf, by which, as he could ſatisfy his own mind, he ſuppoſed he could inſtruct others. The truth is, that, with reſpect to the myſteries of the ſcience, which he ſeems to have known intuitively, he is ſometimes intelligible, and ſometimes otherwiſe; but I have ſuch an opinion of Tartini's penetration and ſaga-

is I know not, but he ſeems perfectly to underſtand Tartini's principles, and to have done juſtice to his genius, without being partial to his defects.

city

city in his musical enquiries, that when he is obscure, I suppose it to be occasioned either by his aiming too much at conciseness in explaining himself, by the insufficiency of common language to express uncommon ideas, or that he soars above the reach of my conceptions; and in this case I am ready to apply to him what Socrates said to Euripides, upon being asked by that poet how he liked the writings of Heraclitus—"What I under-"stand is excellent, which inclines me "to believe that what I do not under-"stand is excellent likewise."

He is succeeded in the church of *St. Antonio* by his scholar, Signor Guglietto Tromba, a young man of merit.

On my arrival at Padua I was extremely desirous of seeing the famous church of Saint Antonio, as well as of hearing the service performed in it; and, supposing my Reader to be possessed of a small portion of my impatience, I shall hasten to give him a short description of this

this fabrick, and an account of its musical establishments.

It is a large old Gothic building, and is called here, by way of excellence, *il Santo*, *the* Saint. It has six domes or cupolas, of which the two largest compose the nave; but though it is only the second church in rank, it is the first in fame and veneration at Padua. It is extremely rich, and so much ornamented, as to appear crowded with paintings and sculpture. At the entrance into the choir the majestic appearance of four immense organs is very striking, of which the front pipes are so highly polished as to have the appearance of burnished silver: the frames too are richly carved and gilt. These four organs are all alike; there are no pannels to the frames, but the pipes are seen on three sides of a square.

There are on common days forty performers employed in the service of this church; eight violins, four violetti or tenors, four violoncellos, four double bafes, and four wind inftruments, with fixteen voices. There are eight *caftrati* in falary, among whom is Signor Gaetano Guadagni, who, for tafte, expreffion, figure, and action, is at the head of his profeffion. His appointment is four hundred ducats a year, for which he is required to attend only at the four principal feftivals. The firft violin has the fame falary. The fecond *foprano*, Signor Cafati, has a feeble voice, but is reckoned to fing with infinite tafte and expreffion. The famous Antonio Vandini is the principal violoncello, and Matteo Biffioli Brefciano the firft hautbois in this felect band.

Signor Francefco Antonio Valloti, the *Maeftro di Capella*, is a native of Piedmont; Dr. Marfili, the worthy profeffor of botany here, to whofe friendly offices, during my ftay at Padua, I have innumerable obligations, did me the favour to introduce me to this eminent mafter. He is efteemed

one

one of the firſt compoſers for the church in Italy; and in the frequent converſations I had with him, I found him to be a good theoriſt as well as practical muſician *. He is a churchman, of the order of St. Francis, near ſeventy years of age; is in poſſeſſion of ſeveral ſcarce and valuable books on the ſubject of muſic, from which he permitted me to make extracts: and was ſo obliging as to ſhew me two large book-caſes filled with the ſcores of his own compoſitions; ſome for voices only, and ſome for voices and inſtruments, among which is the funeral anthem for Tartini; I obtained copies of ſeveral of theſe. He likewiſe communicated to me part of a treatiſe of his own writing, in MS. upon modulation; which, as it is leſs metaphyſical, and has leſs of

* Tartini ſpeaks of Padre Valloti in the following manner, "He was formerly a moſt excellent performer on the organ, as he is now a moſt excellent compoſer, and thorough maſter of his art." *Trattato di Muſica, p.* 100—*Padova* 1754.

mathematics in it than Tartini's Treatiſe, ſo it is more clear, and ſeems more likely to be generally uſeful, if it ſhould be publiſhed.

I was ſorry, upon leaving Padua, to quit this good father, who is of ſo amiable a character, that it is impoſſible to know and not eſteem him. He promiſed me two of his maſſes in ſcore, as ſoon as they could be tranſcribed *, and preſſed me to ſend him a copy of my book when publiſhed; he read my plan with great attention, and over-rated it ſo far as to ſay it was a public concern to Italy.

The theatre of Padua is handſome and convenient; it is approached by two magnificent ſtone ſtair-caſes, and its form is nearly oval. There are in it five rows of boxes; twenty-nine in each, which would perhaps be more pleaſing to the eye if they did not project one over the other.

* Since my arrival in England I have received advice of his having ſent them to Venice, in order to be forwarded to England.

The pit contains one hundred and fifty ſeats, which turn up, and have padlocks fixed to them; the boxes have ſliding ſhutters. Between the grand eſcaliers and the theatre is a room for play, called *Camera di Ridotto*. In June there was a ſerious opera in it, during the fair of St. Anthony; at that time Padua is very gay, and full of company from Venice and the neighbouring cities. The compoſer was Signor Sacchini, a Neapolitan, who is Maſter to the *Conſervatorio* of the *Oſpidaletto* at Venice. The firſt woman was Camilla Mattei, ſiſter to Colomba Mattei, who was in England eight or nine years ago; and the two principal men were Signor Potenza, who was in England at the ſame time as Colomba Mattei, and a famous tenor, *il Cavalier Guglielmi Ettori*, in the ſervice of the Elector of Bavaria, who was more applauded than all the reſt. The two principal dancers were M. Pic, and Signora Binetti; the ſubject of the opera, Scipio in Carthage.

Thurſday, Auguſt 2. This morning I had the honour, in company with Dr. Marſili, to breakfaſt with the Profeſſor of Mathematics, *Padre Colombo*, with whom I had a long converſation relative to Tartini and his poſthumous work, mentioned above.

From hence I went to St. Anthony's church, where, it being *the Day of Pardons*, there was a maſs, with ſolo verſes of *Padre Valloti*'s compoſition, who was there to beat the time; but the two principal ſingers, Signor Guadagni, and Signor Caſati, being abſent, little remains to be ſaid of the execution of this muſic, as far as the vocal was concerned; the writing, however, was good, the harmony pure, the modulation maſterly, and the ſtile grave and ſuitable to the church. But I found that two of the four organs were more than ſufficient to over-power the voices; and *Padre Valloti* told me that the noiſe uſed to be ſtill more intolerable, but that he had reduced, by one at a time, the four

four organs, which were formerly played all at once, to two. The whole four never play now but for the common ſervice, when there are no other performers than the prieſts. The firſt organiſt at preſent, Signor Domenico Locatello, is reckoned an able artiſt*; but it were to be wiſhed that he and his colleague would accompany the voices and inſtruments, which are good, and well worth hearing, with the choir organs only, as we do in England; for, otherwiſe, nothing *but* the organs can be heard: they are, indeed, fine toned inſtruments, but ſo powerful, as to render all the reſt of the performance uſeleſs.

Though it was not a great feſtival, yet the band was more numerous than ordinary. I wanted much to hear the celebrated hautbois Matteo Biſſioli, and the famous old Antonio Vandini, on the violoncello,

* It is but juſtice to ſay that I heard him play the organ alone ſeveral times during the *offertorio*, in a very ſolemn and maſterly manner.

who, the Italians ſay, plays and expreſſes *a parlare*, that is, in ſuch a manner as to make his inſtrument *ſpeak*; but neither had ſolo parts. However, I give theſe two performers credit for great abilities, as they are highly extolled by their countrymen, who muſt, by the frequent hearing of excellent performers of all kinds, inſenſibly become good judges of muſical merit. People accuſtomed to bad muſic, may be pleaſed with it; but thoſe, on the contrary, who have been long uſed to good muſic, and performers, *cannot*. It is remarkable that Antonio, and all the other violoncello players here, hold the bow in the old-faſhioned way, with the hand under it. The choir of this church is immenſe; the baſes are all placed on one ſide, the violins, hautbois, French horns, and tenors on the other, and the voices half in one organ-loft, and half in another; but, on account of their diſtance from each other, the performers were not always exact in keeping time.

The

The day before my departure from Padua, I visited Signor Tromba, Tartini's scholar and successor. He was so obliging as to play several of his master's solos, particularly two which he had made just before his death, of which I begged a copy, regarding these last drops of his pen as sacred relics of so great and original a genius.

VENICE.

I had many enquiries to make, and had very sanguine expectations from this city, with regard to the music of past times as well as the present. The church of St. Marc has had a constant supply of able masters, from the time of Adriano, Zarlino's predecessor, to Galuppi, its present worthy composer. Venice has likewise been one of the first cities in Europe that has cultivated the musical drama or opera: and, in the graver stile, it has been honoured with a Lotti and a

Mar-

Marcello. Add to theſe advantages the *conſervatorios* eſtabliſhed here, and the ſongs of the *Gondolieri*, or Water-men, which are ſo celebrated, that every muſical collector of taſte in Europe is well furniſhed with them, and it will appear that my expectations were well grounded.

The firſt muſic I heard here was in the ſtreet, immediately on my arrival, performed by an itinerant band of two fiddles, a violoncello, and a voice, who, though as unnoticed here as ſmall-coal-men or oyſter-women in England, performed ſo well, that in any other country of Europe they would not only have excited attention, but have acquired applauſe, which they juſtly merited. Theſe two violins played difficult paſſages very neatly, the baſe ſtopped well in tune, and the voice, which was a woman's, was well toned, and had ſeveral eſſentials belonging to that of a good ſinger, ſuch as compaſs, ſhake, and volubility; but I ſhall not mention all the performances of this kind

kind which I met with here; as they happened ſo frequently, the repetition would be tireſome.

This city is famous for its *conſervatorios* or muſical ſchools, of which it has four, the *Oſpidale della Pietà*, the *Mendicanti*, the *Incurabile*, and the *Oſpidaletto a S. Giovanni e Paulo*, at each of which there is a performance every Saturday and Sunday evening, as well as on great feſtivals. I went to that of the *Pietà*, the evening after my arrival, Saturday, Auguſt 4. The preſent *Maeſtro di Capella* is Signor Furlanetti, a prieſt, and the performers, both vocal and inſtrumental, are all girls; the organ, violins, flutes, violoncellos, and even French horns, are ſupplied by theſe females. It is a kind of Foundling Hoſpital for natural children, under the protection of ſeveral nobles, citizens, and merchants, who, though the revenue is very great, yet contribute annually to its ſupport. Theſe girls are maintained here till they are married,

married, and all thoſe who have talents for muſic are taught by the beſt maſters of Italy. The compoſition and performance I heard to-night did not exceed mediocrity; among the ſingers I could diſcover no remarkable fine voice, or performer poſſeſſed of great taſte. However, the inſtruments finiſhed with a ſymphony, the firſt movement of which, in point of ſpirit, was well written and executed.

On Sunday morning, Auguſt 5, I went to the Greek church, which has been tolerated here ever ſince the time of Leo X. The ſervice is performed in the Greek language; the epiſtles and goſpels are chanted by a high-prieſt in a pulpit, and the prayers and reſponſes are ſung in a kind of melody totally different from any other I had ever heard in or out of the church. In this there is no organ, but it is more crowded with ornaments, and its ceremonials are more numerous than in any of the Romiſh churches.

From

From thence I went to St. Marc's, and heard a maſs in muſic, which was ſung by the prieſts, accompanied by the organ only, much in the manner of our full anthems. At St. Luke's church I likewiſe heard part of a maſs with inſtruments; ſome of the tenor voices here were good, and the airs written and ſung with taſte; the muſic was compoſed by a prieſt. There was an excellent fugue in the laſt chorus, well worked and well performed.

In the afternoon of the ſame day I went to the hoſpital *de' Mendicanti*, for orphan girls, who are taught to ſing and play, and on Sundays and feſtivals they ſing divine ſervice in chorus. Signor Bertoni is the preſent *Maeſtro di Capella*. There was a hymn performed with ſolos and choruſſes, and a *mottetto à voce ſola*, which laſt was very well performed, particularly an accompanied recitative, which was pronounced with great force and energy. Upon the whole, the compoſitions had ſome pretty paſſages, mixed

with

with others that were not very new. The ſubjects of the fugues and choruſſes were trite, and but ſlightly put together. The girls here I thought accompanied the voices better than at the *Pietà:* as the choruſſes are wholly made up of female voices, they are never in more than three parts, often only in two; but theſe, when re-inforced by the inſtruments, have ſuch an effect, that the full complement to the chords is not miſſed, and the melody is much more ſenſible and marked, by being leſs charged with harmony. In theſe hoſpitals many of the girls ſing in the counter tenor as low as A and G, which enables them always to keep below the *ſoprano* and *mezzo ſoprano*, to which they ſing the baſe; and this ſeems to have been long practiſed in Italy, as may be ſeen in the examples of compoſition given in the old writers, ſuch as Zarlino, Glariano, Kircher, and others, where the loweſt part of three is often written in the counter-tenor clef.

From

From hence I went to the *Ospidaletto*, of which Signor Sacchini is the maſter, and was indeed very much pleaſed by the compoſition of part of the famous hymn *Salve Regina*, which was ſinging when I entered the church; it was new, ſpirited, and full of ingenious contrivances for the inſtruments, which always *ſaid* ſomething intereſting without diſturbing the voice. Upon the whole, there ſeemed to be as much genius in this compoſition as in any I had heard ſince my arrival in Italy. The performers here too are all orphan girls; one of them, *la Ferrareſe*, ſung very well, and had a very extraordinary compaſs of voice, as ſhe was able to reach the higheſt E of our harpſichords, upon which ſhe could dwell a conſiderable time, in a fair, natural voice.

Even after this, upon the *Piazza di S. Marco*, I heard a great number of vagrant muſicians, ſome in bands, accompanying one or two voices; ſometimes a ſingle voice and guitar; and ſometimes or three guitars together. Indeed it is not to be wondered at, that the ſtreet-muſic here is generally neglected, as people are almoſt ſtunned with it at every corner; but, however, in juſtice to the taſte and diſcernment of the Italians, it muſt be allowed, that when they do admire, it is ſomething excellent; and then, they never "damn with faint praiſe," but expreſs rapture in a manner peculiar to themſelves; they ſeem to agonize with pleaſure too great for the aching ſenſe.

They had here, laſt Carnival, ſeven opera-houſes open at once, three ſerious, and four comic, beſides four play-houſes, and theſe were all crowded every night.

Monday 6. This morning the Doge went in proceſſion to the church of S. *Giovanni e Paolo*. I was not only curious to ſee this proceſſion, but to hear the muſic, which I expected would be very conſiderable, and by a great band; however there was only a maſs ſung in four parts, without other inſtrument than the organ, but then it was ſo good of the kind, ſo well executed and accompanied, that I do not remember to have received more pleaſure from ſuch muſic. One of the organiſts of St. Mark's church, who is in orders, attended, and diſcovered himſelf, in his voluntaries and interludes, to be a very maſterly performer. The voices were well choſen, and well aſſorted, no one ſtronger than the other; the compoſition was of Signor Lotti, and was truly grave and majeſtic, conſiſting of fugues and imitations in the ſtile of our beſt old church ſervices, which have been ſo well ſelected, and publiſhed in ſo magnificent a manner by Dr. Boyce; all was clear and diſtinct, no confuſion or unneceſſary notes; it was even capable of expreſſion, particularly one of the movements, into which the performers entered ſo well, that it affected me even to tears. The organiſt here very judiciouſly ſuffered the voices to be heard in all their purity, inſomuch that I frequently forgot that they were accompanied; upon the whole this ſeems to be the true ſtile for the church: it calls to memory nothing vulgar, light, or prophane; it diſpoſes the mind to philanthrophy, and diveſts it of its groſs and ſenſual paſſions. Indeed my being moved was the mere effect of well-modulated and well-meaſured ſounds, for I knew not the words, which were wholly loſt by the diſtance; nor is this ſpecies of muſic at all favourable to poetry: in the anſwers that are made to the points, the ſeveral parts all ſing different words, ſo that no great effects can be produced by them; but notwithſtanding this defect, ſuch muſic as this, in the ſervice of the church, muſt ever be allowed to have its merit, however it may be exploded, or unfit for theatrical purpoſes.

In conſequence of a meſſage from Mr. Richie, *Chargé des Affaires* to his Britannic Majeſty, to whom Sir James Wright had honoured me with a letter, and who very

very politely and kindly was pleaſed to intereſt himſelf effectually in my ſervice, I was this afternoon favoured with a viſit from Signor Latilla, an eminent compoſer here, and had a long converſation with him relative to the ſubject of my journey. I found him to be a plain, ſenſible man, of about ſixty years of age, who had both read and thought much concerning the muſic of the ancients, as well as that of the moderns, to which he has contributed a conſiderable ſhare for many years paſt *. I admired his candour in adviſing me to go to the *Incurabili*, to hear the girls perform there, with whom he ſaid I ſhould be much pleaſed. They are ſcholars of Signor Galuppi, who is *Maeſtro di Capella* of this Conſervatorio. Unluckily when I arrived there, the performance was begun, however, I had only loſt the

* Moſt of the comic operas performed in London with ſuch ſucceſs, in the time of Pertici and Laſchi, were of Latilla's compoſition; particularly *La Comedia in Comedia*, *Don Calaſcione*, and others. He is uncle to Signor Piccini.

overture, and part of the firſt air. The words were taken from three or four of the Pſalms in Latin, from the hymn *Salve Regina*, and one of the Canticles put into Latin verſe, and in dialogue. I knew not whether I was moſt delighted with the compoſition, or with the execution; both were admirable. Signor Buranello has preſerved all his fire and imagination from the chill blaſts of Ruſſia, whence he is lately returned *. This ingenious, entertaining, and elegant compoſer abounds in novelty, in ſpirit, and in delicacy, and his ſcholars did his muſic great juſtice. Several of them had uncommon talents for ſinging, particularly the *Rota*, *Paſqua Roſſi*, and the *Ortolani*; the two laſt ſung the Canticle in dialogue. The overture, and the whole of this laſt performance were for two orcheſtras. In the overture, which was full of pretty

* Signor Galuppi is beſt known in Italy by the name of *Buranello*, which he acquired from having been born in the little iſland of Burano, near Venice. He is replaced at Peterſburg by Signor Traetta.

paſ-

paſſages, the two bands echoed each other. There were two organs, and two pair of French horns. In ſhort, I was extremely entertained by this performance, and the whole company, which was very numerous, ſeemed equally pleaſed. The young ſingers, juſt mentioned, are abſolute nightingales; they have a facility of executing difficult diviſions equal to that of birds. They did ſuch things in that way, eſpecially the *Rota,* as I do not remember to have heard attempted before. The able maſter was diſcoverable in all the cadences of theſe young ſubjects. The inſtrumental parts were very well executed, and the whole indicated a ſuperior genius in the compoſer and conductor of the performance. This muſic, which was of the higher ſort of theatric ſtile, though it was performed in a church, was not mixed with the church ſervice, and the audience ſat the whole time as at a concert; and, indeed, this might be called a *concerto ſpirituale* with great propriety.

Tueſday 7. This morning there was a maſs in muſic at the church of S. *Gaetano*. It being a great feſtival, all the treaſures and relics were expoſed to public view, and there was a very great crowd. The compoſer of the muſic, and the perſon who beat the time was Signor Menagatto, a prieſt; I cannot ſay that I received much pleaſure from this performance, the organ was coarſe, and poorly played; the voices only two indifferent tenors, and a baſe, and the compoſition very common, and unmarked by any ſtamp of original genius.

The people here, at this ſeaſon, ſeem to begin to live only at midnight. *Then* the canals are crowded with gondolas, and St. Mark's ſquare with company; the banks too of the canals are all peopled, and harmony prevails in every part. If two of the common people walk together arm in arm, they ſeem to converſe in ſong; if there is company on the water, in a gondola, it is the ſame; a mere melody, unaccompanied with a ſecond part, is not to be heard in this city: all the ballads in the ſtreets are ſung in duo. Luckily for me, this night, a barge, in which there was an excellent band of muſic, conſiſting of violins, flutes, horns, baſes, and a kettle-drum, with a pretty good tenor voice, was on the great canal, and ſtopped very near the houſe where I lodged; it was a piece of gallantry, at the expence of an *inamorato* in order to ſenerade his miſtreſs. Shakeſpeare ſays of nocturnal muſic,

"Methinks it ſounds much ſweeter than by day.
"Silence beſtows the virtue on it—I think
"The nightingale, if ſhe ſhould ſing by day,
"When every gooſe is cackling, would be thought
"No better a muſician than the wren."

Whether the time, place, and manner of performing this muſic, gave it adventitious and collateral charms, I will not pretend to ſay; all I know is, that the

 ſympho-

ſymphonies *ſeemed* to me to be admirable, full of fancy, full of fire; the paſſages well contraſted; ſometimes the graceful, ſometimes the pathetic prevailed; and ſometimes, however ſtrange it may be thought, even noiſe and fury had their effect. No one will I believe, at preſent, deny the neceſſity of *diſcord* in the compoſition of muſic in parts; it ſeems to be as much the eſſence of muſic, as ſhade is of painting; not only as it improves and meliorates concord by oppoſition and compariſon, but, ſtill further, as it becomes a neceſſary ſtimulus to the attention, which would languiſh over a ſucceſſion of pure concords. It occaſions a momentary diſtreſs to the ear, which remains unſatisfied, and even uneaſy, till it hears ſomething better; for no muſical phraſe *can end* upon a diſcord, the ear muſt be ſatisfied at laſt. Now, as diſcord is allowable, and even neceſſarily oppoſed to concord, why may not *noiſe*, or a ſeeming jargon, be oppoſed to fixed ſounds

and

and harmonical proportion ? Some of the diſcords in modern muſic, unknown 'till this century, are what the ear can but juſt bear, but have a very good effect as to contraſt. The ſevere laws of preparing and reſolving diſcord, may be too much adhered to for great effects ; I am convinced, that provided the ear be at length made amends, there are few diſſonances too ſtrong for it. If, for inſtance, the five ſounds c. d. e. f. g, are all ſtruck at the ſame inſtant on the harpſichord, provided the d and the f are taken ſoon off, and the three others remain, the ear will not ſuffer much by the firſt ſhock. Or, ſtill further ; if, inſtead of the five ſounds above-mentioned, the following are ſtruck ; c. d ♯. e. f ♯. g. and the d and f # are not held on ſo long as the reſt, all will end to the ſatisfaction of the offended ear.

Wedneſday 8. This day was remarkable for no enquiry relative to the preſent ſtate of muſic in Italy ; however it deſerves

deſerves mention here, on account of the opportunity it afforded me of converſing with the *Abate Martini*, one of the beſt judges of every part of muſic, ancient and modern, that I had yet met with. He is an able mathematician, a compoſer, and performer. He had travelled into Greece, in order to make obſervations in geography, agriculture, and natural hiſtory, but being unable to ſatisfy himſelf as he expected, his pride was ſo hurt by the diſappointment, that he would not publiſh any of his remarks or diſcoveries. Among other curious enquires, he made many concerning the muſic of the modern Greeks, in hopes it would throw ſome light upon that of the ancient. He knows, I believe, as much as any one elſe, about the ſyſtems of Pythagoras, Ptolemy, and the writers collected by Meibomius, as well as of Rameau and Tartini. He is a great admirer of the works of Marcello, and ſings by heart all his cantatas and beſt melodies. After

reading

reading my plan, which we diſcuſſed article by article, he entered much into my views; ſhewed me his Grecian and other manuſcript papers, and I had great reaſon to be ſatisfied both with my reception, and the information with which he favoured me.

9*th*. I had this afternoon another long converſation with the ſame learned gentleman, who was ſo obliging as to bring his manuſcript papers concerning Greek muſic, and to deſire my acceptance of them. I could not help regarding this preſent as a valuable acquiſition, for though the materials it contained were too few for his original purpoſe of forming a book, they appeared likely to be of importance in the courſe of a work, in which it is propoſed to treat not only of ancient muſic, but of the national muſic of moſt parts of the world, from whence ſpecimens, or accounts well authenticated can be had. The *Abate* has, however, collected a ſet of apophthegms or pro-

proverbs, which he intends to publiſh, and which will diſcover the manners and miſery of the modern Greeks, perhaps more effectually than any other work could do.

There was muſic this evening at the church of St. Laurence, compoſed and directed by Signor Sacchini, at which, as it was the vigil of this ſaint, there was a great crowd. I ſuffered, as well as every one elſe, too much by the heat, perhaps, to be eaſily pleaſed, and the compoſition ſeemed rather more common than that I had heard of this ingenious maſter before; however, the vocal parts were not ſo well performed, as there were no other ſingers than thoſe of St. Mark's church, who moſt excel in mere church muſic, accompanied only by the organ. The voices were not good enough for long ſolo parts, nor ſtrong enough to get through a large band; however there were many very pleaſing and agreeable movements, and ſome of the choruſſes

were

were well worked in the fugue and oratorio way. But for this kind of mufic, that of Handel will, I believe, ever ftand fuperior to all other writers; at leaft I have heard nothing yet on the continent of equal force and effect. There is often in the compofitions of others, more melody in the folo parts, more delicacy, and more light and fhade, but as to harmony and contrivance, no one comes near him by many degrees. I muft confefs that I had heard fome of Handel's mufic fo long, and often fo ill performed, that I was fomewhat tired and difgufted with it; but my Italian journey, inftead of lowering the efteem I ever had for the beft writings of that truly great artift, exalted them in my opinion, and at my return renewed my pleafure in hearing them performed. As yet I had heard little but church mufic in Italy; however, in that ftile, *with inftruments*, all other compofitions appeared feeble by comparifon. The fubjects of the fugues were, in gene-

ral,

ral, trivial and common, and the manner of working them dry and artlefs. Indeed the church ftile, *without inftruments*, except the organ, was well known in Italy, and all over Europe, long before Handel's time; and melody is certainly much refined fince: it is more graceful, more pathetic, and even more gay; but for counter-point, fugues, and choruffes of many voices, *with inftruments*, I repeat it, I neither have heard, nor do I ever expect to hear him equalled.

10*th.* This morning I went again to the church of the convent of St. Laurence, where, befides a mafs of Signor Sacchini's compofition, I heard Signor Nazzari, the firft violin of Venice, play a concerto; but we have long heard that inftrument fo well performed upon in England, that nothing is left to admire. However, Signor Nazzari is certainly a very neat and pleafing player; his tone is even, fweet, and full; he plays with great facility and expreffion, and is, upon the

whole,

whole, the beſt ſolo player I had heard on this ſide the Alps.

Argus is ſaid to have had an hundred eyes, and Fame has been painted by the poets *all tongues*; in this place one wiſhes to be all *ears* for muſic, and all *eyes* for painting and architecture. To-day there were ſo many temptations to a lover of harmony, that it was difficult for him to chuſe; for, beſides the four conſervatorios, there were ſeveral *accademias* or private concerts. I was invited to one, which aſſembles on all feſtivals, in order to ſing the works of Marcello, without other accompaniment than a harpſichord; and as this was different from any other I had been at in Italy, I accepted the invitation, though I wiſhed very much to be at the *Incurabili*, where I was ſure of entertainment from Buranello and his ſcholars.

Several of Marcello's Pſalms were here very well ſung by the *Abate Martini* and ſome other *dilettanti*, among whom one

had

had a very good baſe voice, and, between the Pſalms, ſung Marcello's famous cantata called *Caſſandra,* where this compoſer has entirely ſacrificed the muſic to the poetry, by changing the time or ſtile of his movement at every new idea which occurs in the words; this may, perhaps, ſhew a compoſer to be a very ſenſible man, but at the ſame time it muſt diſcover him to be of a very phlegmatic turn, and wholly free from the enthuſiaſm of a creative muſical genius. And, indeed, ſince melody has been allied to grace and fancy, muſical disjointed thoughts on various ſubjects, would be but ill received by the public. One of theſe gentlemen performers was old enough to remember very well the celebrated Benedetto Marcello, who has been dead forty-four years, and gave me ſeveral anecdotes about him; his family, which is noble, ſtill ſubſiſts, and the head of it is now ambaſſador from the Venetian ſtate at the Porte.

11*th*. This afternoon I went again to the *Pietà*; there was not much company, and the girls played a thouſand tricks in ſinging, particularly in the duets, where there was a trial of ſkill and of natural powers, as who could go higheſt, loweſt, ſwell a note the longeſt, or run diviſions with the greateſt rapidity. They always finiſh with a ſymphony; and laſt Wedneſday they played one by Sarte, which I had before heard in England, at the opera of the *Olimpiade*. The band here is certainly very powerful, as there are in the hoſpital above a thouſand girls, and out of theſe there are ſeventy muſicians, vocal and inſtrumental; at each of the other three hoſpitals there are not above forty, as I was informed by Signor L'Atilla, which are choſen out of about a hundred orphans, as the orignal eſtabliſhment requires. But it has been known that a child, with a fine voice, has been taken into theſe hoſpitals before it was bereaved of father or mother. Children are ſometimes brought hither to be educated from the towns belonging to the Venetian ſtate, upon the Continent; from Padua, Verona, Breſcia, and even from other places, ſtill more diſtant; for Franceſca Gabrieli came from Ferrara, and is therefore called the Ferrareſe. The Conſervatorio of the *Pietà* has heretofore been the moſt celebrated for its band, and the *Mendicanti* for voices; but in the voices time and accident may occaſion great alterations; the maſter may give a celebrity to a ſchool of this kind, both by his compoſitions and abilities in teaching; and as to voices, nature may ſometimes be more kind to the ſubjects of one hoſpital than another; but as the number is greater at the *Pietà* than at the reſt, and conſequently the chances of ſuperior qualifications more, it is natural to ſuppoſe that this hoſpital will in general have the beſt band and the beſt voices. At preſent, the great abilities of Signor Galuppi are conſpicuous in the perform-

ances

ances at the *Incurabili*, which is, in point of muſic, ſinging, and orcheſtra, in my opinion, ſuperior to the reſt. Next to that, the *Oſpidaletto* takes place of the other two; ſo that the *Pietà* ſeems to enjoy the reputation of being the beſt ſchool, not for what it *does now*, but for what it *has done*, heretofore.

Sunday 12. This morning, after hearing high maſs well performed at St. Mark's, I went to the patriarchal church of St. Peter, and heard it again there, accompanied by a very fine organ, well played on by one of the prieſts; after that I went to the Franciſcans' church, where one of the Friars likewiſe was organiſt, but he played in a very ſuperior manner, both as to taſte and harmony: though I viſited theſe churches for the ſake of muſic, it was impoſſible to keep my eyes off the pictures and architecture. But it was here I began to find that theſe two objects of ſight were not ſo remote from my chief purpoſe of writing a hiſtory of the pleaſures of the ear, as I at firſt imagined; for I frequently, in the old maſters, met with repreſentations of muſical inſtruments, either of their own times, or at leaſt ſuch as they imagined to be in uſe at the time when the action of the piece happened; thus I obſerved in a famous picture of the Marriage of Cana by P. Veroneſe, in the Sacriſty of S. Georgio Maggiore, a concert, with a variety of inſtruments, of all which I have made a memorandum: and I ſaw this morning, at the Franciſcans, a little picture under the pulpit, by San Croce, which is much admired, and thought to be a good deal in the ſtile of Raphael, in which is a concert of cherubs and ſeraphs; and I obſerved among ſeveral different kinds of lutes and guitars, an inſtrument played with a bow, reſting, like a violin, upon the ſhoulder of the performer, but it had ſix ſtrings.

After I had ſeen theſe, and ſome more churches, I had the honour of a long

con-

conversation with *il Conte Torre Taxis*, who is here a person of great weight *; he is Superintendant-general of the German and Venetian post-office, was a great friend of Tartini, is now in possession of all his MS. compositions, shewed me a great number of them, and has defended his friend in a pamphlet, of which he did me the honour to give me a copy, against some remarks made upon his *Trattato di Musica*, by M. Rousseau, in his *Dict. de Musique*. This nobleman, though young, seems to possess great musical erudition; to have profited from the converse and correspondence of Tartini, and to be an enthusiast for the arts in general. I had great pleasure in his conversation, in which I communicated to him my plan of a History of Music, and was pleased and enlightened by his observations.

* He is of the same family with that German prince, better known in France and England by the name of *Tour Taxis*.

In the afternoon I ſtopped a little while at the new church of the *Jeſuati*, where I heard the organ played with a very uncommon brilliancy of execution, by one of the Dominicans. It was indeed a ſtile of playing more ſuitable to the harpſichord than organ, but, in its way, was very maſterly and powerful. There are ſome reed ſtops in this inſtrument which I had never heard before, and with which the performer produced effects that I was unable to account for. I had not time to make enquiries, as I took this church only in my way to the *Incurabili*, where I was ſo pleaſed, both with the compoſition and performance, that in ſpeaking of them I ſhall find it difficult to avoid hyperboles.

It ſeems as if the genius of Signor Galuppi, like that of Titian, became more animated by age. He cannot now be leſs than ſeventy years old, and yet it is generally allowed here that his laſt operas, and his laſt compoſitions for the church,

abound

abound with more ſpirit, taſte, and fancy, than thoſe of any other period of his life. This evening the Latin Pſalms that were ſung by the orphan girls, gave me great reaſon to concur in the common opinion, for out of ten or twelve movements, there was not one that could be pronounced *indifferent*. There were ſeveral admirable, accompanied recitatives, and the whole abounded with new paſſages, with good taſte, good harmony, and good ſenſe. His accompaniments, in particular, are always ingenious, but, though full, free from that kind of confuſion which diſturbs and covers the voice. I muſt likewiſe do juſtice to the orcheſtra, which is here under the moſt exact diſcipline; no one of the inſtrumental performers ſeemed ambitious of ſhining at the expence of the vocal part, but all were under that kind of ſubordination which is requiſite in a *ſervant* to a *ſuperior*. Of theſe young ſingers I have ſpoken rather warmly before, but in this performance they discovered still new talents and new cultivation. Their music of to-night was rather more grave than that which I had heard here before, and I thought they were more firm in it; that their intonations were more exact, and, as more time was allowed for it, a greater volume of voice by the two principal subjects was thrown out. But in their closes, I know not which astonished me most, the compass of voice, variety of passages, or rapidity of execution; indeed all were such as would have merited and received great applause in the first operas of Europe. I dwell the longer on these performances, as, at present, the theatres of Venice are all shut; but the only difference between this kind of church music, and that of the drama, consists in the chorusses; those of the church are long, elaborate, and sometimes well written. Those who suppose all the church music of Italy to be as light and airy as that of the opera, are mistaken; it is only on festivals that modern

modern mufic can be heard in any of the churches. The mufic of the cathedrals, on common days, is in a ftile as grave and as ancient as that of our church fervices of two hundred years ftanding; and in the parifh churches it is a mere *canto fermo*, or chant, fung in unifon by the priefts only; fometimes with the organ, but more frequently without. If we compare the mufic of Mr. Handel's firft oratorios with the operas he compofed about the fame time, it will appear that the airs of the one are often as gay as thofe of the other. And as to the choruffes of an opera, which are all to be in action, and performed by memory, they muft of courfe be fhorter and lefs laboured than thofe of an oratorio, where every finger has his part before him, and where a compofer is allowed fufficient time to difplay his abilities in every fpecies of what is called by muficians good writing.

From

From the *Incurabili* I had the honour to be carried by his Excellency Signor Murin Giorgi, to an *accademia*, at the *Casa Grimani*, where I first had the pleasure to hear Signora Bassa, a noble Venetian lady. She has long been reckoned the best performer on the harpsichord of all the ladies of Venice; and I found that she played very neatly, and with much taste and judgment. The company consisted of the chief nobility of Venice, the three persons I have named being among the first class. They did great justice in this assembly to the abilities of Mrs. Cassandra Wynn, from England, who was there last year, and had left behind her the character of a very great player.

Tuesday 14. This evening being the vigil of the Assumption, there were musical performances at three different churches. I went first to that of the *Celestia*; the vespers were composed and directed by the *Maestro* of the Pietà, Signor

Signor Furlanetto; there were two orchestras, both well filled with vocal and instrumental performers: the overture was spirited, and the first chorus good, in *Contra Punto*; then there was a long symphony in dialogue, between the two orchestras, and an air well accompanied, though but indifferently sung. After this an air in dialogue with the chorus, which had a good effect: an air for a tenor voice, of little merit, and one for a base, which was ingeniously put together, making use by turns of all the principal instruments: I did not stay out the whole performance, but what I heard seemed superior to any composition that I had before met with of this author; he availed himself of the two orchestras, and produced several effects which, with one, would have been impracticable.

From hence I went to the *Ospidaletto*, where the music and musicians spoke a different language. The performance was a Latin oratorio; *Machabæorum Mater*; the

the muſic was by Signor Sacchini; there were ſix characters in it, the principal was performed by Franceſca Gabrieli: it was divided into two parts; the firſt was over before I arrived, for which I was very ſorry, as what remained delighted me extremely, both as to the compoſition, which was excellent, and the ſinging which had infinite merit. When I entered the church the *Ferrareſe* was ſpeaking an admirable accompanied recitative in ſuch a manner as is ſeldom heard; it was terminated by a *Bravura* air, with a pathetic ſecond part in Jomelli's oratorio ſtyle, but by no means in his paſſages; there was then a recitative and ſlow air by Laura Conti, who is poſſeſſed of no great power of voice; it is a mere *voce di Camera*; but ſhe has infinite expreſſion and taſte, and charmed me in a different way: then followed another recitative, and after it a duet, which was truly ſublime; it was extremely well executed by Domenica Paſquati and Ippolita

Ippolita Santi; upon the whole, Signor Sacchini rifes in my opinion, and according to my feelings and intelligence he is the fecond in Venice, having no fuperior there but Signor Galuppi. The finging I heard at this hofpital to-night would, as well as that of the *Mendicanti,* I am certain, receive great applaufe in the firft opera of Europe.

Wednefday 15. I went this morning to St. Mark's church, at which, being a feftival, the doge was prefent. I there heard high mafs performed under the direction of Signor Galuppi, compofer of the mufic. Upon this occafion there were fix orcheftras, two great ones in the galleries of the two principal organs, and four lefs, two on a fide, in which there were likewife fmall organs. I was placed very advantageoufly in one of the great organ lofts, with Signor L'Atilla, affiftant to Signor Galuppi *. The mu-

* This inftrument has pedals, and but one row of box keys.

fic,

ſic, which was in general full and grave, had a great effect, though this church is not very happily formed for muſic, as it has five domes or cupolas, by which the ſound is too much broken and reverberated before it reaches the ear.

From hence I went again to the *Celeſtià*, which church was very much crowded. The maſs was ſet to muſic by Signor Furlanetto, maſter to the *Pietà*: the reſources of this compoſer are very few; he has little fire and leſs variety, but he ſins more on the ſide of genius than learning, as his harmony is good, and modulation regular and warrantable; but I muſt own, that his muſic is to me tireſome, and leaves behind it a languor and diſſatiſfaction; whereas that of Signor Galuppi and Sacchini always exhilerates and enlivens. Signor Nazari played here a concerto on the violin in a very neat and pleaſing manner. I know not of whoſe compoſition, but it was by no means remarkable for novelty. After dinner I went

went to the church of Santa Maria Maggiore to ſee ſome pictures, and ſtumbled on muſic, but ſuch muſic as I did not think it poſſible for the people of Italy to bear. The organ was out of tune, other inſtruments out of time, and the voices were both; then the compoſition ſeemed juſt ſuch ſtuff as a boy who was learning counter-point would produce after the firſt two or three leſſons. After I had ſeen the two beſt pictures in the church, the famous St. John the Baptiſt, by Titian, and Noah's ark by Giacomo Baſſano, I ran away from this muſic to the *Incurabili*, where Buranello's nightingales, the Rota, and Paſqua Roſſi, poured balm into my wounded ears. There was not much company, and the girls did not exert themſelves; however, after what I had juſt heard, their performance was raviſhing; and it was not without regret that I reflected upon this being the *laſt time* I ſhould hear it.

Thurſday 16. My viſit to Signor Galuppi this morning was long, profitable, and entertaining. I was very glad to find upon ſeeing him, that time had ſpared the perſon as well as genius of this excellent compoſer. He is ſtill lively and alert, and likely to delight the lovers of muſic many years. His character and converſation are natural, intelligent, and agreeable. He is in figure little and thin, but has very much the look of a gentleman. Signor Galuppi was a ſcholar of the famous Lotti, and very early taken notice of as a good harpſichord player, and a genius in compoſition. He was ſo obliging as to preſent me to Signora Galuppi; to ſhew me his houſe; an admirable picture of a ſleeping child, by P. Veroneſe, which has been long in his wife's family; and to carry me into his working-room, with only a little clavichord in it, where, he told me, he *dirtied paper*. His family has been very large, but all his children, except three

three or four, are now well married. He has the appearance of a regular family man, and is eſteemed at Venice as much for his private character as for his public talents. He ſeems, however, rather hurt at the encouragement and protection which ſome eccleſiaſtical dunces, among whom is F——, meet with as compoſers here. Indeed, except Sacchini, his ſecond, he ſtands ſo high among the preſent race of muſicians in Venice, that he ſeems a giant among dwarfs: he was ſo obliging, at my requeſt, as to promiſe me a piece of his compoſition, which has not yet been made public, as a relick and mark of his friendſhip. I ſhewed him my plan, and we talked over that, and muſic and muſicians, very cordially, and with ſimilar ſentiments: his definition of good muſic I think admirable, and though ſhort, very comprehenſive. It conſiſts, he ſays, of *vaghezza, chiarezza, e buona modulazione**. He and Signor L'A-

* Beauty, clearneſs, and good modulation.

tilla, among many other particulars, recollected the names of all the great masters of the conservatorios, and had patience to let me write them down. These gentlemen likewise informed me that the expence of the conservatorios, on account of music, is very inconsiderable, there being but five or six masters to each for singing and the several instruments, as the elder girls teach the younger. The *Maestro di Capella* seldom does more than compose and direct: sometimes, indeed, he writes down *closes*, and usually attends the last rehearsal and first public performance.

A succession of able masters has constantly been employed in these schools: Hasse was once *Maestro* to the *Incurabili*, and has left a *Miserere*, which is still performed there in Passion Week, and is, according to the Abate Martini, a wonderful composition *.

* I obtained, before I left Venice, a copy of it; and since my arrival in England, I have been honoured

Signor Galuppi ſeemed to have full employment here, even in ſummer, when there are no operas, as he is firſt *Maeſtro di Capella* of St. Mark, and of the *Incurabili*. He has a hundred zechins a year as domeſtic organiſt to the family of Gritti, and is organiſt of another church, of which I have forgot the name. He certainly merits all that can be done for him, being one of the few remaining original geniuſſes of the beſt ſchool perhaps that Italy ever ſaw. His compoſitions are always ingenious and natural, and I may add, that he is a good contrapuntiſt, and a friend to poetry. The firſt appears by his ſcores, and the latter by the melodies he ſets to words, in which the expreſſion of his muſic always correſponds with the ſenſe of the author, and often improves it. His compoſitions for the church are but little

honoured with a letter from Count Bujovich, of Venice, with ſeveral intereſting particulars relative to the riſe and progreſs of theſe muſical inſtitutions.

known in England; to me they appear excellent *; for though many of the airs are in the opera ſtile, yet, upon occaſion, he ſhews himſelf to be a very able writer in the true church ſtile, which is grave, with good harmony, good modulation, and fugues well worked.

I was this evening at a ſecond *Accademia*, at Signor Grimani's, which was much more conſiderable than the firſt. Signor Sacchini was there, and ſeveral of the principal muſicians of Venice. La Signora Regina Zocchi, a lady who had her muſical education at the *Incurabili*, under the celebrated Signor Haſſe, and who is now well married, and received, and even courted by the firſt people here, ſung: ſhe has a very powerful voice, and good ſhake, with great volubility and expreſſion. D. Flaminio Tomj, who has a mere *Voce di Camera*, ſung

* I procured at Venice, ſome of his motets; and Giaſeppe, an excellent copieſt there, undertook to tranſcribe, and ſend after me, two or three of his maſſes.

with

with exquifite tafte. La Signora Baffa performed on the harpfichord, two or three concertos with much grace and precifion. Add to this, that the whole was well heard by a very large company, compofed of the firft nobility of Venice, among whom was Signor Mocenigo, fon to the prefent doge.

Friday 17. I had this morning the honour of a fecond interview with Count Torre Taxis, during which, I had the pleafure to hear his excellency perform on the harpfichord, of which inftrument he is an able mafter; he played voluntaries for a confiderable time, in which he difcovered much fkill in modulation, and I found him worthy of a place on the upper form of the *Tartini* fchool. He fhewed me a great number of maffes, motets, and oratorios of his compofition, for though young, he is already a very voluminous writer. He is poffeffed of a very curious keyed inftrument which was made at Berlin, under the direction of his Pruffian Majefty: it is, in fhape, like a large clavichord, has feveral changes of ftops, and is occafionally a harp, a harpfichord, a lute, or piano forte; but the moft curious property of this inftrument is, that by drawing out the keys the hammers are transferred to different ftrings, by which means a compofition may be tranfpofed half a note, a whole note, or a flat third lower at pleafure, without the embarraffment of different notes or clefs, real or imaginary.

Among the *Dilettanti* here, befides Count Taxis, there is a noble Venetian, Signor Giovan Cornaro, remarkable for his genius and fkill in compofition: he had compofed a mafs for a great feftival at a church in Padua, which was performed there, while I was at Venice, with an immenfe band of voices and inftruments.

This evening, in order to make myfelf more fully acquainted with the na-

ture

ture of the confervatorios, and to finifh my mufical enquiries here, I obtained permiffion to be admitted into the mufic fchool of the *Mendicanti*, and was favoured with a concert, which was performed wholly on my account, and lafted two hours, by the beft vocal and inftrumental performers of this hofpital: it was really curious to *fee*, as well as to *hear* every part of this excellent concert, performed by females, violins, tenors, bafes, harpfichord, French horns, and even double bafes; and there was a priorefs, a perfon in years, who prefided: the firft violin was very well played by Antonia Cubli, of Greek extraction; the harpfichord fometimes by Francefca Roffi, *maeftra del coro*, and fometimes by others; thefe young perfons frequently change inftruments. The finging was really excellent in different ftiles; Laura Rifegari and Giacoma Frari, had very powerful voices, capable of filling a large theatre; thefe fung *bravura* fongs, and capital fcenes felected from Italian operas; and Francefca Tomj, fifter to the Abate of that name, and Antonia Lucuvich, whofe voices were more delicate, confined themfelves chiefly to pathetic fongs, of tafte and expreffion. The whole was very judicioufly mixed; no two airs of a fort followed each other, and there feemed to be great decorum and good difcipline obferved in every particular; for thefe admirable performers, who are of different ages, all behaved with great propriety, and feemed to be well educated. It was here that the two celebrated female performers, the Archiapate, now Signora Guglielmi, and Signora Maddalena Lombardini Sirmen, who have received fuch great and juft applaufe in England, had their mufical inftructions. If I could have ftaid a few days longer at Venice, I might have enjoyed the fame kind of entertainment at the other three confervatorios, having been tempted to continue there by fuch an offer from a friend

friend who had intereſt ſufficient to procure me a ſight of the *interior diſcipline* of theſe admirable muſical ſeminaries; and I declined this obliging offer with the greater reluctance, as there is not in all Italy, any eſtabliſhment of the ſame kind; but being willing to divide the time I had allowed myſelf for the enquiries I had to make there as equally as poſſible, I reſiſted that temptation as well as ſeveral other offers with which I was honoured, from ſome of the principal nobility, of being admitted to their private concerts; and thus far for the honour of Italy, as well as for my own, I muſt ſay, that I met with the politeſt treatment, and greateſt encouragement and aſſiſtance imaginable, wherever I ſtopt. At Venice my expectations were greatly ſurpaſſed, as I had always been told that the inhabitants, particularly the better ſort, were reſerved and difficult of acceſs.

I was indebted for much of my entertainment and information at Venice, to the assiduity and friendship of Mr. Edwards, a young gentleman who was born in England, but has lived so long in this city, that he has wholly lost his vernanacular tongue. With this gentleman, and D. Flaminio Tomj, I went from the Conservatorio of the *Mendicanti*, to Signor Grimani's: here the Abate Tomj sung two or three pathetic airs with more taste than I can remember to have heard since the death of Palma. There was a great deal of company, and the musical performances of various kinds continued till two or three o'clock in the morning; at which time I took a melancholy leave of Signor Grimani, who had honoured me with something more than mere politeness and hospitality: in a less elevated character I should venture to call it friendship, but here it could only be condescending goodness.

To

To finiſh my account of the muſic of this charming city, I muſt obſerve, that though the compoſers of the Venetian ſchool are in general good contrapuntiſts, yet their chief characteriſtics are delicacy of taſte, and fertility of invention; but many circumſtances concur to render the muſic of Venice better, and more general than elſewhere. The Venetians have few amuſements but what the theatres afford; walking, riding, and all field-ſports, are denied them. This in ſome degree accounts for muſic being ſo much, and in ſo coſtly a manner, cultivated; the number too of theatres, in all which the Gondoliers have admiſſion gratis, may account for the ſuperior manner in which they ſing compared with people of the ſame claſs elſewhere *. And in the private families, into which the girls of

* When a box belonging to a noble family is diſengaged, and likely to remain empty, the opera manager permits the Gondolieri to occupy it, rather than a report ſhould prevail that the performance drew but little company.

the Conſervatorios marry, it is natural to ſuppoſe that good taſte and a love for muſic are introduced.

The library of St. Mark here, which abounds with books in all other faculties, afforded me but few materials on the ſubject of muſic. However I gained conſiderably by the converſation of Signor Zanetti, the firſt librarian, who was very polite and communicative.

Printing has been carried on in Venice with great ſpirit, ever ſince the year 1459, when it was eſtabliſhed there by Nicholas Janſen; and there is perhaps no city in Italy in which ſo many books have been publiſhed. At preſent the preſs is very active and fertile, and the number of bookſellers in the fine ſtreet called *Merceria* is very conſiderable. I found in no one place ſo many old authors on the ſubject of muſic as here; and as to the new, I met with many that I was unable to find elſewhere, particularly the firſt volume of Padre Martini's Hiſtory

Hiſtory of Muſic. The principal bookſellers in Venice are Paſquali, Remondini, Bettinelli, Occhi, and Antonio di Caſtro.

The art of engraving muſic there ſeems to be utterly loſt, as I was not able to find a ſingle work printed in the manner we print muſic in England. In the firſt place there is no ſuch thing as a muſic *ſhop* throughout Italy, that I was able to diſcover. Indeed M. di Caſtro, a ſpirited bookſeller, one of the four abovementioned, has publiſhed a propoſal for printing muſic with types, in the manner attempted by Mr. Fought, but has met with ſmall encouragement, having only publiſhed one book of little duets and trios. Muſical compoſitions are ſo ſhort-lived in Italy, ſuch is the rage for novelty, that for the few copies wanted, it is not worth while to be at the expence of engraving, and of the rolling-preſs. Indeed there, as in Turkey, the buſineſs of a tranſcriber furniſhes employment for ſo many people, that it is cruel to wiſh to rob them of it, eſpecially as that trade ſeems more briſk and profitable than any other.

As a ſupplement to the article Venice, I muſt add, that, ſince my return to England, I have been favoured with a letter from thence, dated January 25, 1771, containing the following particulars relative to the ſtate of muſic there, at that time. " At the theatre of S. Benetto we " have had repreſented, during the pre-" ſent carnival, the opera of Alexander " in India; compoſed by Signor Bertoni, " maſter of the *Mendicanti*, which has " been univerſally applauded; particu-" larly a duet, ſung by Signora de Amicis " and Signor Caſelli. At the ſame " theatre we have at preſent *il Siroe ri-" conoſciuto*, compoſed by Signor Borghi, " which is generally diſliked.

" The muſic, at the opera-houſe of S. " Moisè, pleaſes very much; notwith-" ſtanding it is ſo ill executed, that the " author, Signor Garzaniga, a Neapoli-" tan, has great reaſon to be mortified, " though crowned with general praiſe."

BOLOGNA.

BOLOGNA.

My chief errand in this city was to ſee and converſe with the learned *Padre Martini*, and the celebrated Signor *Farinelli*, the former being regarded by all Europe as the deepeſt theoriſt, and the other as the greateſt practical muſician of this, or perhaps of any age or country; and, as I was ſo fortunate as to be well received by both, I ſhall make no apology for being minute in my account of two ſuch extraordinary perſons.

Padre Martini is a Franciſcan, and Maeſtro di Capella of the church belonging to that order in Bologna. He has many years been employed in writing the Hiſtory of Muſic, of which the firſt volume only has, as yet, been publiſhed. Two editions, one in folio, and one in quarto, were printed at the ſame time in Bologna, 1757; a ſecond volume is in the preſs, and he propoſes finiſhing the work in five volumes. The firſt volume

is

is chiefly employed in the Hiſtory of Muſic among the Hebrews; the ſecond and third will compriſe that of the ancient Greeks; the fourth the Latin or Roman muſic, with the hiſtory of muſic in the church; the fifth and laſt volume will be appropriated to modern muſic, with ſome account of the lives and writings of the moſt famous muſicians, and engravings of their heads. We reciprocally agreed upon an open and cordial correſpondence, and a mutual promiſe of confidence and aſſiſtance; but it is greatly to be lamented that the good Father Martini is far advanced in years, and is of an infirm conſtitution, having a very bad cough, ſwelled legs, and a ſickly countenance; ſo that there is reaſon to fear he will hardly have life and health ſufficient to complete his learned, ingenious, and extenſive plan.

It is impoſſible, by reading his book, to form a judgment of the character of this good and worthy man. As yet

he

he has treated only the drieſt and moſt abſtruſe part of the ſubject, in which he had great opportunities to ſhew his reading and knowledge, which are deep and extenſive, but none to diſplay the excellence of his character, which is ſuch as inſpires not only reſpect but kindneſs. He joins to innocence of life, and ſimplicity of manners, a native chearfulneſs, ſoftneſs, and philanthropy. Upon ſo ſhort an acquaintance I never liked any man more; and I felt as little reſerve with him in a few hours, as with an old friend or beloved brother; it was impoſſible for confidence to be more cordial, eſpecially between two perſons whoſe purſuits were the ſame: it is however true, that though they are the ſame with reſpect to the object, they are different with reſpect to the way: I had advanced too far to retreat before I could procure his book, and when I had found it, my plan was ſo much digeſted as to render the adoption or imitation of any other very inconvenient. Befides, as every object may be approached by a different route, it may alfo be feen in a different point of view; two different perfons therefore may exhibit it with equal truth, and yet with great diverfity: I fhall avail myfelf of P. Martini's learning and materials, as I would of his fpectacles, I fhall apply them to my fubject, as it appears to me, without changing my fituation; and fhall neither implicitly adopt his fentiments in doubtful points, nor tranfcribe them where we agree.

Befides his immenfe collection of printed books, which has coft him upwards of a thoufand zechins, P. Martini is in poffeffion of what no money can purchafe, MSS. and copies of MSS. in the Vatican and Ambrofian libraries, and in thofe of Florence, Pifa, and other places, for which he has had a faculty granted him by the Pope, and particular permiffion from others in power. He has ten different copies of the famous Micrologus of

Guido

Guido Aretinus, and as many made from different manuſcripts of John de Muris, with ſeveral other very ancient and valuable MSS. He has one room full of them; two other rooms are appropriated to the reception of printed books, of which he has all the ſeveral editions extant; and a fourth to practical muſic, of which he has likewiſe a prodigious quantity in MS. The number of his books amounts to ſeventeen thouſand volumes, and he is ſtill encreaſing it from all parts of the world *. He ſhewed me ſeveral of his moſt curious books and MSS. upon which I communicated to him the catalogue of mine. He was ſurpriſed at ſome

* I had frequently ſurpriſed ſeveral bookſellers on the continent with the liſt of my books on the ſubject of muſic, but, in my turn, I was now ſurpriſed. Though Padre Martini has had many preſents made him of ſcarce books and MSS. yet he has often paid a great price for others, particularly for one written in Spaniſh, 1613, which coſt him a hundred ducats, about twenty guineas, at Naples, where it was printed.

of them, and ſaid they were extremely rare; of theſe he took down the titles, and, at my ſecond viſit, he was pleaſed to think my plan worth borrowing to tranſcribe, which he did with his own hand.

Thurſday, Auguſt 23. It will give pleaſure to every lover of muſic, eſpecially thoſe who have been ſo happy to have heard him, that Signor Farinelli ſtill lives, and is in good health and ſpirits. I found him much younger in appearance than I expected. He is tall and thin, but by no means infirm in his appearance. Hearing I had letter for him, he was ſo obliging as to come to me this morning at Padre Martini's, in whoſe library I ſpent a great part of my time here. Upon my obſerving, in the courſe of our converſation, that I had long been ambitious of ſeeing two perſons, become ſo eminent by different abilities in the ſame art, and that my chief buſineſs at Bologna was to gratify that ambition, Signor Farinelli,

point-

pointing to P. Martini, ſaid, "What *he* "is doing will laſt, but the little that I "have done is already gone and forgot- "ten." I told him, that in England there were ſtill many who remembered his performance ſo well, that they could bear to hear no other ſinger; that the whole kingdom continued to reſound his fame, and I was ſure tradition would hand it down to the lateſt poſterity.

Friday 24. This being St. Bartholomew's day, I went to the church of that name, where I was told the muſic would be good; however, I found it quite the contrary. Signor Gibello was *Maeſtro di Capella*, and ſeveral *caſtrati* ſung, but neither the compoſition nor execution pleaſed me; the compoſition had not one of Buranello's three requiſites, *vaghezza, chiarezza, e buona modulazione*, to recommend it, and the execution was ſlovenly and incorrect.

Though there was no opera in Bologna at this time, yet, for the ſake of ſeeing the theatre, I went to the play. The houſe is elegant, but not large; it has however five rows of boxes, twelve or thirteen on a ſide. When I went in I knew not what the play would be, but expected a ribbald farce, as uſual; when, to my great ſurpriſe, I found it was an Italian tragedy, called *Tomire,* written by Padre Ringhieri. I had never ſeen one before, and was much pleaſed with the opening, but ſoon grew tired of the long ſpeeches and declamation; they were paſt all bearing tedious. Thomyris, Queen of the Amazons, came on dreſſed in a very equivocal manner; for, in order to give her a martial look, ſhe had her petticoats truſſed up in front above her knees, which were very diſcernible through her black breeches. However ſtrange this appeared to me, the audience clapped violently, as they did conſtantly at the worſt and moſt abſurd things in the piece. There was a great deal of religion in it, and ſuch anachroniſms, that

that they talked of J. C. and the Trinity, nor were Free-will and Predeſtination forgotten; and when Cyrus is dying of the wound he received in battle, he is examined by a Jewiſh prieſt (a principal character in the play) as his confeſſor, concerning his religious principles, and he makes to him a *profeſſion of faith.*

This kind of ſpectacle has been ſo long neglected in Italy, that it ſeems to have been wholly loſt; and now, after a ſecond birth, appears to be in its *infancy*. However, the Italian language is certainly capable of great things; as it can ſupport dignity without the trammels of rhyme. The actors too are good, as to propriety and variety of geſture; but in voice, a monotony reigns here, as in the Italian pulpit. The paſſion for dramas in muſic has ruined true tragedy as well as comedy in this country; but the language and genius of the people are ſo rich and fertile, that when they become heartily tired of muſic, which by exceſs of it they will probably be very ſoon, the ſame rage for novelty, which has made them fly with ſuch rapidity from one ſtile of compoſition to another, often changing from a better to a worſe, will drive them to ſeek amuſement from the ſtage, *without* muſic. And in that caſe, when they apply all their powers to the ſock and buſkin, and the writer and actor are obliged to make uſe of every reſource with which the national language and genius abound; they will probably ſurpaſs the reſt of Europe in the dramatic, as well as in other arts. But before this can happen, much muſt be done towards refining the national taſte, which is at preſent too much depraved by farce, buffoonery, and ſong. The inattention, noiſe, and indecorum of the audience too, are quite barbarous and intolerable. The ſilence which reigns in the theatres of London and Paris, during repreſentation, is encouraging to the actor, as well as deſirable to the hearer of judgment and feeling. In Italy the

the theatres are immenſe, and, in order to be heard through ſpace and noiſe, the actors ſeem in a perpetual bawl. Each ſentence, thus pronounced, is more like the harangue of a general at the head of an army of a hundred thouſand men, than the ſpeech of a hero or heroine in converſation; this allows of but few modulations of voice; all the paſſions are alike noiſy, the tender and the turbulent.

The ſcenes and decorations in this piece were elegant and judicious: there was one ſcene in particular very ſtriking; it was that of a high, but fertile mountain, from which Thomyris deſcended with her court and guards, in order to come to a parley with Cyrus.

The orcheſtra was rather weak and ordinary; and, in general, I found the muſic in the ſtreets here worſe, and leſs frequent then at Venice. However, I was ſaluted ſoon after my arrival at the inn, as every ſtranger is, with a duet, very well played by by a violin and mandoline; and, this afternoon, an itinerant band played under my window ſeveral ſymphonies and ſingle movements of execution, extremely well, in four parts.

Saturday 25. This day I had the pleaſure to ſpend with Signor Farinelli, at his houſe in the country, about a mile from Bologna, which is not yet quite finiſhed, though he has been building it ever ſince he retired from Spain *. Il Padre Maeſtro Martini was invited to dine there with me, and I cannot reſiſt the deſire of confeſſing that I was extremely happy at finding myſelf in the company of two ſuch extraordinary men.

Signor Farinelli has long left off ſinging, but amuſes himſelf ſtill on the harp-

* The country is flat all round him, but though the environs of this city are perhaps the moſt fertile of any in Italy, yet the inhabitants ſeem poſſeſſed of nothing like *taſte*, in laying out their gardens; however, Signor Farinelli's houſe commands a fine proſpect of Bologna, and of the little hills near it.

ſichord and viol d' amour: he has a great number of harpſichords made in different countries, which he has named according to the place they hold in his favour, after the greateſt of the Italian painters. His firſt favourite is a *piano forte*, made at Florence in the year 1730, on which is written in gold letters, *Rafael d'Urbino*; then, Coreggio, Titian, Guido, &c. He played a conſiderable time upon his Raphael, with great judgment and delicacy, and has compoſed ſeveral elegant pieces for that inſtrument. The next in favour is a harpſicord given him by the late queen of Spain, who was Scarlatti's ſcholar, both in Portugal and Spain; it was for this princeſs that Scarlatti made his two firſt books of leſſons, and to her the firſt edition, printed at Venice, was dedicated, when ſhe was princeſs of Aſturias: this harpſichord, which was made in Spain, has more tone than any of the others. His third favourite is one made likewiſe

likewiſe in Spain, under his own direction; it has moveable keys, by which, like that of Count Taxis, at Venice, the player can tranſpoſe a compoſition either higher or lower. Of theſe Spaniſh harpſichords the natural keys are black, and the flats and ſharps are covered with mother of pearl; they are of the Italian model, all the wood is cedar, except the bellies, and they are put into a ſecond caſe.

Signor Farinelli was very converſible and communicative, and talked over old times very freely, particularly thoſe when he was in England; and I am inclined to believe, that his life, were it well written, would be very intereſting to the public, as it has been much chequered, and ſpent in the firſt courts of Europe; but, as I hope it is yet far from finiſhed, this ſeems not to be the place to attempt it: however, the following anecdotes, chiefly picked up in converſation with himſelf

himſelf and Padre Martini, may perhaps for the preſent, gratify in ſome meaſure, the curioſity of the reader.

Carlo Broſchi, called Farinelli, was born at Naples in 1705; he had his firſt muſical education from his father, Signor Broſchi, and afterwards was under Porpora, who travelled with him; he was ſeventeen when he left that city to go to Rome, where, during the run of an opera, there was a ſtruggle every night between him and a famous player on the trumpet, in a ſong accompanied by that inſtrument: this, at firſt, ſeemed amicable and merely ſportive, till the audience began to intereſt themſelves in the conteſt, and to take different ſides: After ſeverally ſwelling out a note, in which each manifeſted the power of his lungs, and tried to rival the other in brilliancy and force, they had both a ſwell and a ſhake together, by thirds, which was continued ſo long, while the audience eagerly waited the event, that both

both ſeemed to be exhauſted; and, in fact, the trumpeter, wholly ſpent, gave it up, thinking, however, his antagoniſt as much tired as himſelf, and that it would be a drawn battle; when Farinelli, with a ſmile on his countenance, ſhewing he had only been ſporting with him all this time, broke out all at once in the ſame breath, with freſh vigour, and not only ſwelled and ſhook the note, but ran the moſt rapid and difficult diviſions, and was at laſt ſilenced only by the acclamations of the audience. From this period may be dated that ſuperiority which he ever maintained over all his cotemporaries.

In the early part of his life he was diſtinguiſhed throughout Italy, by the name of *the boy*.

From Rome he went to Bologna, where he had the advantage of hearing Bernacchi, (a ſcholar of the famous Piſtocco, of that city) who was then the

firſt

firſt ſinger in Italy, for taſte and knowledge; and his ſcholars afterwards rendered the Bologna ſchool famous.

From thence he went to Venice, and from Venice to Vienna; in all which cities his powers were regarded as miraculous; but he told me, that at Vienna, where he was three different times, and where he received great honours from the Emperor Charles the VI. an admonition from that prince was of more ſervice to him than all the precepts of his maſters, or examples of his competitors for fame: his Imperial Majeſty condeſcended to tell him one day, with great mildneſs and affability, that in his ſinging, he neither *moved* nor *ſtood ſtill* like any other mortal; all was ſupernatural. "Thoſe gigantic ſtrides, (ſaid he); thoſe "never-ending notes and paſſages *(ces "notes qui ne finiſſent jamais)* only ſur-"priſe, and it is now time for you to "pleaſe; you are too laviſh of the gifts "with which nature has endowed you; "if

“ if you wiſh to reach the heart, you “ muſt take a more plain and ſimple “ road.” Theſe few words brought a-bout an entire change in his manner of ſinging; from this time he mixed the pathetic with the ſpirited, the ſimple with the ſublime, and, by theſe means, delighted as well as aſtoniſhed every hearer.

In the year 1734, he came into England, where every one knows who heard, or has heard of him, what an effect his ſurpriſing talents had upon the audience; it was extacy! rapture! enchantment!

In the famous air *Son qual Nave,* which was compoſed by his brother, the firſt note he ſung was taken with ſuch delicacy, ſwelled by minute degrees to ſuch an amazing volume, and afterwards diminiſhed in the ſame manner, that it was applauded for full five minutes. He afterwards ſet off with ſuch brilliancy and rapidity of execution, that it was difficult for the violins of thoſe days to keep pace with him. In ſhort, he was to all other ſingers as ſuperiour as the famous horſe Childers was to all other running-horſes; but it was not only in ſpeed, he had now every excellence of every great ſinger united. In his voice, ſtrength, ſweetneſs, and compaſs; in his ſtile, the tender, the graceful, and the rapid. He poſſeſſed ſuch powers as never met before, or ſince, in any one human being; powers that were irreſiſtible, and which muſt ſubdue every hearer; the learned and the ignorant, the friend and the foe.

With theſe talents he went into Spain in the year 1737, with a full deſign to return into England, having entered into articles with the nobility, who had then the management of the opera, to perform the enſuing ſeaſon. In his way thither he ſung to the king of France at Paris, where, according to Riccoboni, he enchanted even the French themſelves, who at that time univerſally abhorred Italian muſic; but the firſt day he performed before the king and queen of Spain, it was determined that he ſhould be taken into the ſervice of the court, to which he was ever after wholly appropriated, not being once ſuffered to ſing again in public. A penſion was then ſettled on him of upwards of 2000 l. ſterling a year.

He told me, that for the firſt ten years of his reſidence at the court of Spain, during the life of Philip the Vth, he ſung every night to that monarch the ſame four airs, of which two were compoſed by Haſſe, *Palido il ſole,* and *Per queſto dolce Ampleſſo.* I forget the others, but one was a minuet which he uſed to vary at his pleaſure.

After the death of Philip the Vth, his favour continued under his ſucceſſor Ferdinand the VIth, by whom he was dignified with the order of *Calatrava* in 1750; but then his duty became leſs conſtant and fatiguing, as he perſuaded this prince to have operas, which were a great

great relief to him: he was appointed ſole director of thoſe ſpectacles; and had from Italy, the beſt compoſers and ſingers of the time, and Metaſtaſio to write. He ſhewed me in his houſe four of the principal ſcenes in *Didone* and *Netette*, painted by Amiconi, who accompanied him firſt into England, and then into Spain, where he died.

When the preſent king of Spain aſcended the throne, he was obliged to quit that kingdom, but his penſion is ſtill continued, and he was allowed to bring away all his effects. The furniture of his houſe is very rich, as it is almoſt entirely compoſed of the preſents he received from great perſonages. He ſeems very much to regret the being obliged to ſeek a new habitation, after having lived twenty-four years in Spain, where he had formed many friendſhips and connections that were dear to him; and it is a great proof of the prudence and moderation of his character, that in a country and court,

 where

where jealouſy and pride are ſo predominant, he continued ſo long to be the king's chief favourite, a diſtinction odious to every people, without the leaſt quarrel or difference with any of the Spaniards.

When he returned into Italy in 1761, all his old friends, relations, and acquaintance were either dead or removed from the places where he had left them; ſo that he had a ſecond life to begin, without the charms of youth to attach new friends, or his former talents to gain new protectors.

He ſays that Metaſtaſio and he were twins of public favour, and entered the world at the ſame time, he having performed in that poet's firſt opera. When he ſhewed me his houſe, he pointed out an original picture, painted about that time, by Amiconi, in which are the portraits of Metaſtaſio, of Farinelli himſelf, of Fauſtina, the famous ſinger, and of Amiconi.

From his converſation, there is reaſon to believe, that the court of Spain had fixed on Bologna for his reſidence; though the Italians ſay his firſt deſign was to ſettle at Naples, the place of his birth, but that he was driven from thence by the numerous and importunate claims of his relations; however that may be, he has a ſiſter and two of her children with him, one of whom is an infant, of which he is doatingly fond, though it is croſs, ſickly, homely, and unamiable; yet this is a convincing proof, among others, to me that he was deſigned by nature for family attentions and domeſtic comforts: but in converſation he lamented his not being able, for political reaſons, to ſettle in England; for, next to Spain, that was the place in the world, he ſaid, where he ſhould have wiſhed to ſpend the remainder of his days.

He ſpeaks much of the reſpect and gratitude he owes to the Engliſh. When I dined with him it was on an elegant ſervice

vice of plate, made in England at the time he was there. He ſhewed me a number of pictures of himſelf, painted during that time, from one of which by Amiconi, there is a print. He has an Engliſh ſweep-chimney boy playing with a cat, and an apple-woman with a barrow, by the ſame hand: he has likewiſe a curious Engliſh clock, with little figures playing in concert on the guitar, the violin, and violoncello, whoſe arms and fingers are always moved by the ſame pendulum.

His large room, in which is a billiard-table, is furniſhed with the pictures of great perſonages, chiefly ſovereign princes, who have been his patrons, among whom are two emperors, one empreſs, three kings of Spain, two princes of Aſturias, a king of Sardinia, a prince of Savoy, a king of Naples, a princeſs of Aſturias, two queens of Spain, and Pope Benedict the XIVth. In other apartments are ſeveral charming pictures, by Zimenes and Morillo,

rillo, two Spanifh painters of the firft eminence, and Spagnolet.

Sir Benjamin Keene was a great favourite with him, and he fpeaks of his death, not only as a misfortune to the two courts of England and Spain, but as an irreparable lofs to himfelf and all his friends. He fhewed me feveral pictures painted in England, in the manner of Teniers, by a man, during the time he was in prifon for debt; I forget his name; thefe, he faid, Lord Chefterfield had given him in the politeft manner imaginable.

Upon my expreffing fome defire to write his life, or, at leaft, to infert particulars of it in my hiftory. "Ah," fays he, by a modefty rather pufhed too far, "if you have a mind to compofe a good "work, never fill it with accounts of fuch "defpicable beings as I am." However, he furnifhed me with all the particulars concerning Domenico Scarlatti, which I defired, and dictated to me very obligingly, while I entered them in my pocket-book.

He ſtill retains a few words of the Engliſh language, which he had picked up during his reſidence in London, and entertained me a great part of the day with accounts of his reception and adventures there. He repeated a converſation he had with Queen Caroline, about Cuzzoni and Fauſtina; and gave me an account of his firſt performance at court to his late majeſty George the IId. in which he was accompanied on the harpſichord by the princeſs royal, afterwards princeſs of Orange, who inſiſted on his ſinging two of Handel's ſongs at ſight, printed in a different clef, and compoſed in a different ſtile from what he had ever been uſed to. He told me of his journey into the country with the Duke and Ducheſs of Leeds, and with Lord Cobham; of the feuds of the two operas; of the part which the late Prince of Wales took with that managed by the nobility; and the Queen

and

and Princeſs Royal with that which was under the direction of Handel.

He likewiſe confirmed to me the truth of the following extraordinary ſtory, which I had often heard, but never before credited. Seneſino and Farinelli, when in England together, being engaged at different theatres on the ſame night, had not an opportunity of hearing each other, till, by one of thoſe ſudden ſtage-revolutions which frequently happen, yet are always unexpected, they were both employed to ſing on the ſame ſtage. Seneſino had the part of a furious tyrant to repreſent, and Farinelli that of an unfortunate hero in chains; but, in the courſe of the firſt ſong, he ſo ſoftened the obdurate heart of the enraged tyrant, that Seneſino, forgetting his ſtage-character, ran to Farinelli and embraced him in his own.

Monday 22. This day, after viſiting the Inſtitute, I waited on the *Dottoreſſa Madame Laura Baſſi*, and met with a very polite

polite and eaſy reception. Upon naming Padre Beccaria, and ſhewing his recommendation in my tablets, we were inſtantly good friends. This lady is between fifty and ſixty; but though learned, and a genius, not at all maſculine or aſſuming. We talked over the moſt celebrated men of ſcience in Europe. She was very civil to the Engliſh, in eulogiums of Newton, Halley, Bradley, Franklin, and others. She ſhewed me her electrical machine and apparatus: the machine is ſimple, portable, and convenient; it conſiſts of a plain plate of glaſs, placed vertically; the two cuſhions are covered with red leather; the receiver is a tin forked tube; the two forks, with pins at the ends, are placed next the glaſs plate. She is very dextrous and ingenious in her experiments, of which ſhe was ſo obliging as to ſhew me ſeveral. She told me that Signor Baſſi, her huſband, immediately after Dr. Franklin had proved the identity of electrical fire and lightning, and publiſhed his method of preſerving buildings from the effects of it, by iron rods, had cauſed conductors to be erected at the Inſtitute; but that the people of Bologna were ſo afraid of the rods, believing they would bring the lightning upon them, inſtead of the contrary, that he was forced to take them down. Benedict XIV. one of the moſt enlightened and enlarged of the popes, a native, and in a particular manner the patron, as well as ſovereign of Bologna, wrote a letter to recommend the uſe of theſe conductors; but it was ſo much againſt the inclination of the inhabitants of this city, that Signor Baſſi deſiſted entirely, and they have never ſince that time been uſed here.

There is an apparatus, and a room apart for electricity at the Inſtitute, but the machines are old, and very inferior to thoſe in uſe at this time in England. It is remarkable that this univerſity has no correſpondence with England, nor is it able to purchaſe our Philoſophical

losophical Transactions. The salaries are small, and the money allowed for the support of the Institute is all appropriated. This I was told by the Keeper or *Custode*, who shewed me the apartments. My visit with the learned Signora Bassi was very agreeable, and she was so obliging as to offer me a letter to Signor Fontana at Florence, one of the first mathematicians in Europe.

They speak much at Bologna of the *Brav' Orbi*, or blind fidlers, who were not in town when I was there; but all the masters admire them, in their way, very much, particularly Iomelli, who always sends for them, when in the same town, to play to him. They travel about in summer to Rome, Naples, and elsewhere; one plays on the violin, the other on the violoncello, and is called *Spacca Nota*, or Split Note.

Tuesday being a festival, mass was performed in music at the church of the convent of St. Augustin. The composer

was

was Signor Caroli, *Maestro di Capella del Duomo* of Bologna, There was a great band, but neither learning, tafte, or novelty to recommend the mufic. It confifted of old paffages, ftrung together in a heavy manner, without even the merit of a little pertnefs now and then to enliven it. And what rendered this mufic ftill more tirefome, was the finging, which was rather below mediocrity.

In the afternoon I went to take a melancholy leave of the Cavalier Farinelli. He kindly importuned me to ftay longer at Bologna, and even chid me for going away fo foon. I found him at his Raphael, and prevailed on him to play a good deal: he *fings* upon it with infinite tafte and expreffion. I was truly forry to quit this extraordinary and amiable perfon: he preffed me to write to him, if there was any thing in Italy which he could procure or do for me. I ftaid with him till it was fo late, that I was in danger of being fhut out of the city of Bologna, the gates being

ing locked every night as ſoon as it is dark.

By the advice of P. Martini I ſtaid at Bologna two days longer than I intended, in order to be preſent at a kind of trial of ſkill among ſuch compoſers of this city as are members of the celebrated Philharmonic Society, founded in 1666.

There is an annual exhibition, or public performance, morning and evening, on the thirtieth of Auguſt, in the church of *S. Johanni in Monte**. This year the *Principe*, or Preſident, was Signor Petronio Lanzi. The band was very numerous, conſiſting of near a hundred voices and inſtruments. There are two large organs in the church, one on each ſide

* This church is rendered famous by the poſſeſſion of two of the beſt pictures in Bologna, or, perhaps, in the world, the St Cecilia of Raphael, and the Madonna of the Roſary of Dominichini. They are placed in two chapels, oppoſite to each other, between which, and in full view of theſe charming paintings, I had the advantage of ſitting to hear the muſic.

of

of the choir; and, besides these, a small one was erected for the occasion, in front, just behind the composer and singers. The performers were placed in a gallery, which formed a semi-circle round the choir.

In the *Messa* or Morning Service the *Kyrie* and *Gloria* were composed by Signor Lanzi, President for the second time. His music was grave and majestic; it opened with an introduction, by way of overture, of a considerable length, which afterwards served as an accompaniment to the voices in a very good chorus: there were likewise in it several pleasing airs, and a well-written fugue.

The *Graduale* was composed by Signor Antonio Caroli, in the same dry, uninteresting stile as the performance mentioned above, which would have been thought trite and dull sixty years ago.

The *Credo* was composed by Signor Lorenzo Gibelli, a scholar of Padre Martini,

tini, which, in point of harmony, had its merit.

The morning ſervice was finiſhed by a ſymphony, with ſolo parts, by Signor Gioanni Piantanida, principal violin of Bologna, which really aſtoniſhed me. This performer is upwards of ſixty years of age, and yet has all the fire of youth, with a good tone, and modern taſte; and, upon the whole, ſeemed to me, (though his bow-hand has a clumſy and aukward look) more powerful upon his inſtrument than any one I had, as yet, heard in Italy.

In the *Veſpero*, or evening ſervice, the *Domine* was compoſed by Signor Anto. Fontana di Carpi, a prieſt, and was a pleaſing performance, of one movement only.

The Abate Gio. Caliſto Zanotti, nephew to the learned librarian of that name, compoſed the *Dixit*; and in this performance there were all the marks of an original and cultivated genius. The move-

movements, and even paſſages were well contraſted; and, to make uſe of the language of painters, there were diſcernible in it, not only light and ſhade, but even *mezzo tints*. He proceeded from one thing to another by ſuch eaſy and inſenſible gradations, that it ſeemed wholly the work of nature, though conducted with the greateſt art. The accompaniments were judicious, the ritornels always expreſſed *ſomething*, the melody was new and full of taſte, and the whole was put together with great judgment, and even learning. In ſhort, I have very ſeldom in my life received greater pleaſure from muſic than this performance afforded me; and yet the vocal parts were but indifferently executed, for at this time there were no great ſingers at Bologna, though there were two or three that were agreeable, particularly a *contr' alto*, Signor Cicognani, who, in a ſerious opera, would be a gcod ſecond ſinger; and a *ſoprano*, Conſoli, a boy of about thirteen or fourteen, with a very ſweet, but feeble voice, who poſſeſſed great taſte and expreſſion. Signor Zanotti is a ſcholar of Padre Martini, and one of the *Maeſtri di Capella* in the church of S. Petronio.

The next compoſer who took upon him the direction of the orcheſtra (every author beat time to his own performance) was Signor Gabrielle Vignali. His part of the ſervice was the *Confitebor*, which he had ſet in ſuch an inoffenſive manner, that the niceſt judge could not be hurt by its faults, nor the moſt envious critic by its beauties.

Beatus Vir was ſet by D. Giuſeppe Coretti, a venerable prieſt, who ranks very high in Bologna as a *contrapuntiſt*; indeed his muſic was very maſterly, and, in ſound harmony, and regular modulation, had infinite merit.

Laudato Puer was compoſed by Signor Bernardo Ottani, another ſcholar of P. Martini, who is young, and a promiſing compoſer. There were many ingenious

pretty

pretty things in his performance, as well as in that which followed, which was a hymn by D. Francefco Orfoni, a young prieft, and fcholar likewife of P. Martini.

The whole was concluded by the *Magnificat* of Signor Antonio Mazzoni, fecond mafter of the *duomo* or cathedral, who is compofer to the opera here, and has been in that character at Naples, Madrid, and Peterfbourg. He is faid to have great fire and fancy, but in this performance, which was all chorus, they were not difcoverable; the whole was founded upon a ground-bafe, which was played by all the inftruments, and feemed laboured and conftrained.

There were prefent at this exhibition all the critics of Bologna, and the neighbouring cities, and the church was extremely crowded. Upon the whole, I was very well entertained; and the variety of ftile, and mafterly compofition were fuch as reflected honour, not only upon the Philharmonic Society, but upon the city of Bologna itſelf, which has, at all times, been fertile in genius, and has given birth to a great number of men of abilities in all the arts.

I muſt acquaint my muſical reader, that at the performance juſt mentioned, I met with M. Mozart and his ſon, the little German, whoſe premature and almoſt ſupernatural talents aſtoniſhed us in London a few years ago, when he had ſcarce quitted his infant ſtate. Since his arrival in Italy he has been much admired at Rome and Naples; has been honoured with the order of the *Speron d'Oro*, or Golden Spur, by his Holineſs, and was engaged to compoſe an opera at Milan for the next Carnival.

I cannot quit this city without returning once more to the good Padre Martini. After the muſical performance above deſcribed, I went, by appointment, to his convent to bid him adieu, as I was to quit Bologna early next morning. He waited

waited for me in his ſtudy, it being late, and beyond the monaſtic hours of ſeeing company. He had kindly prepared for me recommendatory letters for Florence, Rome, and Naples; and had looked out ſtill more curious books to ſhew me, of which I took the titles, in hopes of meeting with them ſome time or other. He had told me, the day before, that, as he ſhould not be preſent at the Philharmonic Meeting, he ſhould rely on my judgment and account, how matters went off and were conducted; and now deſired me to deſcribe to him every ſingle piece. After doing this very faithfully, I was going to retire, when he ſays, "Won't you ſtay "for the words to be written to theſe "Canons?"—I had the day before ſung with a young Franciſcan, his ſcholar, out of a prodigous large MS. book of his Canons, ſeveral very pleaſing ones for two voices only, of which I ſeemed to expreſs a deſire to have one or two copied, and this excellent father remembering it, had ſet a perſon to work for me, who was writing when I entered the ſtudy; but, as he had uſually two or three *amanuenſes* there, I did not mind him *. At length we parted, on my ſide with ſorrow, and on his with a recommendation to write to him often.

FLORENCE.

This city has been longer in poſſeſſion of muſic, if the poets and hiſtorians may be credited, than any other in Europe. Dante, a Florentine, born in 1265, ſpeaks of the organ and lute as inſtruments well known in his time; and has taken an opportunity to celebrate the talents of his friend Caſella, the muſician, in the ſecond canto of his *Purgatorio*.

The hiſtorian Villani, cotemporary with Petrarca, ſays that his *canzonets* were

* Padre Martini has compoſed an amazing number of ingenious and learned *canons*, in which every kind of intricacy and contrivance, that ever had admiſſion into this difficult ſpecies of compoſition, has been happily ſubdued.

uni-

univerſally ſung in Florence, by the old and the young of both ſexes. And we are told that *Lorenzo il Magnifico*, in Carnival time, uſed to go out in the evening, followed by a numerous company of perſons on horſeback, maſked, and richly dreſſed, amounting ſometimes to upwards of three hundred; and the ſame number on foot, with wax tapers burning, which rendered the ſtreets as light as at noon day, and gave a ſplendour to the whole ſpectacle. In this manner they marched through the city, till three or four o'clock in the morning, ſinging, with *muſical harmony*, in four, eight, twelve, and even fifteen parts, accompanied with various inſtruments, ſongs, ballads, madrigals, and catches, or ſongs of humour, upon ſubjects then in vogue; and theſe, from being performed in Carnival time, were called *Canti Carnaſcialeſchi*. *

* They were firſt collected and publiſhed by Franceſco Spaziano. Florence, 1559.

But even before this period the company of *Laudiſti*, or Pſalm-ſingers, was formed, which has continued ever ſince; it is now called *La Compagnia*, and the morning after my arrival in Florence, between ſix and ſeven o'clock, they paſſed by the inn where I lodged, in grand proceſſion, dreſſed in a whitiſh uniform, with burning tapers in their hands. They ſtopped at the *duomo*, or great church, juſt by, to ſing a chearful hymn, in three parts, which they executed very well. In this manner, on Sundays and holidays, the trades-people and artiſans form themſelves into diſtinct companies, and ſing through the ſtreets, in their way to church. Thoſe of the pariſh of S. Benedetto, we are informed by Creſcimbeni, were famous all over Italy; and at the great Jubilee, in the beginning of this century, marched through the ſtreets of Rome, ſinging in ſuch a manner as pleaſed and aſtoniſhed every body.

September 3. I went to the little theatre *di via Santa Maria*, to hear the comic opera of *La Peſcatrice*, compoſed by Signor Piccini. There are but four characters in this drama, two of which were repreſented by Signora Giovanna Baglioni, and her ſiſter Coſtanza, whom I had heard at Milan; the other two were Signor Paolo Bonaveri, a good tenor, and Signor Goſtantino Ghigi. Giov. Baglioni appeared here to much greater advantage than at Milan, where the theatre is of ſuch a ſize as to require the lungs of a Stentor to fill it. She ſung very well; her voice is clear, and always in tune, her ſhake open and perfect, and her taſte and expreſſion left nothing to wiſh in the ſongs ſhe had to ſing. She was extremely applauded; the houſe was very much crowded, the band was good, and the muſic worthy of Signor Piccini; full of that fire and fancy which characteriſe all the productions of that ingenious and original compoſer.

In the duomo, or cathedral here, which is one of the largeſt churches in Italy, there is the fineſt toned organ I ever heard; whether, like St. Paul's, in London, it is meliorated by the magnitude and happy conſtruction of the building, I cannot tell, but it pleaſed me exceedingly. It has moreover, the advantage of being very well played on by Signor Matucci, the preſent organiſt, whoſe ſtile is not only grave and ſuitable to the church, but learned in modulation, and, in ſlow movements, truly pathetic.

M. de Maupertuis, in his voyage to the polar circle, was told by the Laplanders of a monument which they regarded as the moſt wonderful thing in their country: upon the merits of this report only, he ſays, he was almoſt aſhamed to confeſs that he undertook a very fatiguing and dangerous journey to ſee it. Something of the ſame kind happened to me: in going to the opera, a ſecond time, I was ſurprized to find the theatre almoſt empty; and,

and, upon enquiry into the reaſon of it, I was told that the chief muſicians, and the beſt company of Italy, were aſſembled at Figline, a town in the Upper Val d'Arno, about thirty miles from Florence, to celebrate a kind of jubilee, in honour of Santa Maſſimina, the protectreſs of that place; and I am almoſt aſhamed to confeſs, that, without enquiring of perſons well informed, I took upon truſt this report, and travelled all night, in order to be preſent at theſe games the next day.

I arrived at the place of action about ſeven o'clock in the morning, and found the road and town very full of country people, as at a wake in England, but ſaw very few carriages, or perſons of rank and faſhion; however, conſiderable preparations were making in the great ſquare, for the diverſions of the evening.

At eleven high maſs was performed in the principal church, which was very much ornamented, and illuminated with innumerable

innumerable wax tapers, which, together with the greateſt crowd I ever was in, rendered the heat almoſt equal to that of the black-hole at Calcutta, and the conſequences muſt have been as fatal, had not the people been permitted to go out as others preſſed in; but neither religious zeal, nor the love of muſic, could keep any one long in the church who was able to get out. In ſhort, the whole was a ſtruggle between thoſe whoſe curioſity made them ſtrive to enter the church, and others whoſe ſufferings and fear made them uſe every means in their power to get out.

By permitting myſelf to drive with the ſtream, I at length was carried to a tolerable place near one of the doors, where I had perſeverance ſufficient to remain during the whole ſervice, as I was in conſtant expectation of being rewarded for my ſufferings, by the performance of ſome great ſinger, whom I had not heard be-

fore;

fore; but in this I was disappointed, as all the vocal performers, except one*, were very indifferent: the music, however, was very pretty; full of taste and fancy: it was composed by Signor Feroce, Fiorentino. The principal violin was played by Signor Modele, who, with his son, played very neatly a duet concerto: after this the Abate Fibbietti sung a motet with such taste in the slow movements, and fire in the quick, as were truly astonishing; his voice was sweet and clear, his intonations perfectly true; his expression and fancy charming, and he left nothing to wish, but a shake a little more open.

At four o'clock in the evening, the games began in the great square, which is a large piece of ground of an oblong form. There were 1500 peasants of the neighbourhood employed upon this occasion, who had been three months in train-

* The Abate Fibbietti, an excellent tenor.

ing: they had the ſtory of David and Goliah to repreſent, which was done with the moſt minute attention to the ſacred ſtory, and the *coſtume* of the ancients. The two armies of the Iſraelites and Philiſtines met, marching to the ſound of ancient inſtruments, ſuch as the *crotolo* or cymbal, the ſyſtrum, and others: they were all dreſſed *à l'Antique*, even to the common men; the kings, princes, and generals, on both ſides, were ſumptuouſly clad, and all on horſeback, as were ſeveral hundreds of the troops.

The giant, Goliah, advanced and gave the challenge: the Iſraelites retreated in great conſternation, till, at length, little David appears, and entreats Saul to let him be his champion, which requeſt, after ſome time is granted; the reſt of the ſtory was well told, and it was ſo contrived, that after Goliah was ſtunned by the ſtone from David's ſling, in cutting off his head with the Giant's own great ſword, a quantity of blood guſhed out, and many of of the ſpectators ſhricked with horror, ſuppoſing it to be the blood of the perſon who repreſented the champion of the Philiſtines. After this, there was a pitched battle between the two armies, and the Iſraelites, being victorious, brought David in triumph, at the head of the priſoners and ſpoils of the enemy, mounted on a ſuperb chariot, in the ancient form.

At Veſpers I heard the ſame ſtory *ſung* in an oratorio, ſet by the Abate Feroce, in which Signor Fibbietti, the tenor, had a capital part, to which he did great juſtice: during this performance, the whole town was illuminated in an elegant manner, and there were very ingenious fireworks played off in the great ſquare; and, in juſtice to the pacific diſpoſition of the Tuſcans, I muſt obſerve, that though there were at leaſt 20,000 people aſſembled together on this occaſion, without guards, yet not the leaſt accident or diſturbance happened. This may perhaps be be owing, in ſome meaſure, to the peculiar ſobriety of the Italians, as I do not remember to have ſeen one drunken perſon during the whole time I was in Italy.

It being impoſſible to procure a bed, if I would have paid eight or ten zechins for it, and the night being very fine, I ſet out at eleven o'clock for Florence, where I arrived at four the next morning: and though the muſical performance at Figline was not what I had been made to expect, yet the reſt was very ſuperior, and what I was not likely to meet with elſewhere; ſo that, upon the whole, I did not think the time ſpent in this excurſion entirely loſt.

Wedneſday, *Sept*. 6. I was preſent at the performance of another opera, ſet by Piccini, called *Le Donne Vendicate*. There were in this drama but four characters, which were repreſented very well by the ſame perſons as thoſe in the *Peſcatrice*. There are but two acts in any of the comic

mic operas I have yet ſeen in Italy; but the dances, which are likewiſe two, may be called *balli pantomimi*, or pantomime entertainments, as they are each as long almoſt as an act of the opera. There are two or three charming airs in this burletta. Coſtanza Baglioni ſung extremely well; and the tenor, who is a favourite here, was very much applauded; but though a good ſinger, I neither think his voice or taſte equal to thoſe of Signor Lovatini.

Friday, Sept. 7. In the evening I heard veſpers performed at the church of the Annunciation, by a great number of ſingers, prieſts and laymen, accompanied only by a little organ, a violoncello, and two double baſes. The muſic was in the old choral ſtile of the ſixteenth century. After this *full* performance, in the great choir, there was other ſinging in different chapels of this beautiful church, by boys placed in different organ lofts, who were accompanied by tenor and base voices below.

Saturday, Sept. 8. This morning, there were no other instruments to accompany the voices than those which I had heard at the same church yesterday, though the day was a great festival: however, the vocal performers were more numerous, and they sung a mass in eight parts, four on a side, very well; it was composed by Orazio Benevoli, of the Roman school, who flourished soon after Palestrina, and, for that time, and that kind of music, is excellent. There are no regular fugues, the subjects are changed with the words, and little or no effect is produced by the melody, when divided among so many parts; but the points and imitations *must* be short, or the movement would be endless. However, the effect of the *whole*, to lovers of harmony, is admirable. After the services were ended, Signor Veroli, a very good soprano, sung a grave motet

a voce

a voce ſola. He is uſually the firſt ſinger in the ſerious opera here, and has a very pleaſing voice, with a conſiderable ſhare of taſte. The motet was compoſed by Padre Dreyer, *Maeſtro di Capella* of the *Annunciata.* He was formerly a famous ſinger at Dreſden, with a *ſoprano* voice, but on account of the too great notice which was taken of him, by a perſon of diſtinction there, he was ſent away, and has been many years eſtabliſhed in this city: he is now in years; I had a long converſation with him, and found him very intelligent and obliging. He ſays, the muſic of Paleſtrina is uſed here on all days, except feſtivals; and, upon my requeſting him to favour me with a copy of the moſt celebrated compoſition performed in his church, he told me that it was the *Miſerere* of *Allegri,* which is ſung here, as in the Pope's chapel, only on Good Fridays, and that it ſhould be tranſcribed for me immediately: but as I had already obtained a copy of that famous compofition from Padre Martini, who had one made by the exprefs order of the late Pope, I declined the acceptance of his obliging offer.

In the evening I went again to the opera of *Le Donne Vendicate*, which I mention only becaufe it gives me an opportunity of remarking the extraordinary good humour of an Italian audience; for this being the laft night of the prefent company's performance, the crowd and applaufe were prodigious; printed fonnets, in praife of fingers and dancers, were thrown from the flips, and feen flying about the houfe in great numbers, for which the audience fcrambled with much eagernefs, and at the clofe of all, it was rather acclamation than applaufe.

Sunday, Sept. 9. This morning I was at a very folemn fervice in the convent *delle Monache*, or nuns of the *Portico*, about a mile from Florence. This performance coft upwards of 300 zechins; it it was the laſt conſecration of eight nuns; the archbiſhop was there, a great deal of the firſt company of Florence, and a very numerous band of vocal and inſtrumental performers. I had here the pleaſure of hearing Signor Manzoli. In the firſt part of the maſs, there was a trio between him, Signor Veroli, and the ſecond *maeſtro* of the Nunziata, whoſe voice is a Baritono. The muſic of the maſs was by Signor Soffi, of Lucca, but he not being preſent, Signor Veroli beat time to the choruſſes. Beſides the verſes which Signor Manzoli ſung in the maſs, with which I was very much delighted, though his voice ſeemed leſs powerful, even in a ſmall church, than when he was in England; he performed a charming motet, compoſed by Signor Monza, of Milan.

Signor Guarducci, and Signor Ricciarelli, left Florence a few days only before my arrival there, otherwiſe I might have heard a duo ſung by Signor Manzoli and Signor Guarducci, who performed together at a private concert: this was a loſs the more to be regretted, as theſe two great performers are ſeldom in the ſame place, and very rarely ſing together.

At preſent, though Florence does not abound in muſical geniuſſes of it's own growth, yet it is very well ſupplied from other places; for, beſides the performers above mentioned, Signor Campioni is ſettled here, as *maeſtro di Capella* to the grand duke; Signor Dottel, the celebrated performer on the German flute, is of his band, and Signor Nardini is engaged here, as principal violin, in the ſervice of the ſame prince *.

I heard likewiſe in this city a good performer on the double harp, Signora Anna Fond, from Vienna, who is in the ſervice of the court; and my little countryman, Linley, who had been two years under

* Theſe three eminent maſters, whoſe merit is well known to all Europe, have been lately tempted to quit Leghorn, by the munificence of the grand duke.

Signor Nardini, was at Florence when I arrived there, and was univerſally admired. The *Tommaſino*, as he is called, and the little Mozart, are talked of all over Italy, as the moſt promiſing geniuſſes of this age.

The comedy of *il Saggio Amico*, by Goldoni, which I had ſeen at Breſcia, was repreſented this evening at another theatre, larger and more ſplendid than that where I had ſeen the burlettas. I found ſo much company there, that it was impoſſible to procure a ſeat: the play was dull, but there was a Turkiſh dance between the acts, which laſted near half an hour: it was very ingenious, and the ſcenes and dreſſes were the moſt magnificent I had ever ſeen in my life *.

In my way to this theatre, juſt as it was growing dark, I met in the ſtreets a company of *Laudiſti*: they had been at Fieſole, and were proceeding in proceſſion to their own little church. I had

* The price for the pit in this theatre, and for that of every comic opera in Italy, is one paul, amounting to almoſt ſix pence Engliſh.

the curiofity to follow them, and procured a book of the words they were finging*. They ftopt at every church in their way, to fing a ftanza in three parts; and when they arrived at their own church, into which I gained admiffion, there was a band of inftruments to receive them, who, between each ftanza that they fung, played a fymphony. They performed vefpers in *Canto Fermo*, affifted by their chaplain: the whole was conducted with great decorum, and was certainly a very innocent amufement. Some of the companies of *Laudifti*, in Florence, have fubfifted near five hundred years. I found a folio MS. of *Laudi Spirituali*, with the notes, in the Magliabecchi library, compofed for the company of friars of the order of the *Umiliati*, and fung at the church of All Saints, Florence, 1336.

Monday, *Sept*. 10. This afternoon, I had

* The title of thefe hymns runs thus, *Laudi da Cantarfi da Fratelli della venerabil Compagnia di S. M. Maddalena de' pazzi e S. Guifeppe in S. Maria in Campidoglio in Firenze*, 1770.

had the pleaſure of hearing Signor Nardini, and his little ſcholar Linley, at a great concert, at the houſe of Mr. Hempſon, an Engliſh gentleman, where there was much company. This gentleman plays the common flute in a particular manner, improving the tone very much, by inſerting a piece of ſpunge into the mouth-piece, through which the wind paſſes. He performed two or three difficult concertos, by Haſſe, and Nardini, very well. There was a perſon from Perugia, who played a ſolo on the viol d'amore, very agreeably; and Signor Nardini played both a ſolo and a concerto, of his own compoſition, in ſuch a manner as to leave nothing to wiſh: his tone is even and ſweet; not very loud, but clear and certain; he has a great deal of expreſſion in his ſlow movements, which, it is ſaid, he has happily caught from his maſter Tartini. As to execution, he will ſatisfy and pleaſe more than ſurprize: in ſhort, he ſeems the completeſt player on

the

the violin in all Italy; and, according to my feelings and judgment, his ſtile is delicate, judicious, and highly finiſhed*.

The Tommaſino Linley played two concertos, very much in the manner of his maſter. Signor Nardini has a great number of young profeſſors under his care, as his maſter, Tartini, uſed to have, among whom is a ſon of Mr. Agus, from England.

Tueſday 11. At another great *accademia*, at the houſe of Signor Domenico Baldigiani, I this evening met with the famous *Improvviſatrice*, Signora Maddalena Morelli, commonly called *La Corilla*, who is likewiſe a ſcholar of Signor Nardini, on the violin; and afterwards I was frequently at her houſe†. Beſides

* Whoever has heard the poliſhed performance of the celebrated Madame Sirmen, may form a pretty juſt idea of Signor Nardini's manner of playing.

† She has, almoſt every evening, a *converſatione*, or aſſembly, which is much frequented by the foreigners, and men of letters, at Florence.

her

her wonderful talent of ſpeaking verſes *extempore* upon any given ſubject, and being able to play a *ripieno* part, on the violin, in concert, ſhe ſings with a great deal of expreſſion, and has a conſiderable ſhare of execution.

I was ſeveral times at the houſe of Signor Campioni, whoſe trios have been ſo well received in England. He is married to a lady who paints very well, and who is likewiſe a neat performer, on the harpſichord. He has the greateſt collection of old muſic, particularly Madrigals, of the ſixteenth and ſeventeenth centuries, Padre Martini's excepted, that I ever ſaw: he has likewiſe himſelf compoſed a great deal for the church, ſince his eſtabliſhment at Florence. He ſhewed me the ſcore of a *Te Deum*, which he ſet for the birth of the grand duke's eldeſt daughter, full of curious canons, and ingenious contrivances: it was performed by a band of two hundred voices and inſtruments.

Among

Among the *Dilettanti*, at Florence, the Marquis of Ligniville is regarded as a good theorist and composer. He has set the hymn *Salve Regina* in *Canon*, for three voices. The music is neatly engraved, and copies of it are given to his friends. The Marquis was not in Florence during my residence there; however, I was presented with a copy of this curious piece, by a musician in the service of his excellence *.

Mr. Perkins, an English gentleman, who has resided a considerable time in this city and in Bologna, is likewise a good musician. A letter from Padre

* In the title page of this *Salve Regina*, the Marquis of Ligniville is stiled Prince of Conca, chamberlain to their Imperial Majesties, director of the music of the court in Tuscany, and member of the philharmonic society of Bologna. He is Prince of Conca, in the kingdom of Naples, by right of his mother; is son of the famous Marshal Ligniville, who was killed in the gardens of Colorno, a country house belonging to the Duke of Parma, during the war of 1733.

Martini

Martini procured me the honour of his acquaintance. This gentlemen is entitled to my beſt acknowledgments for many muſical curioſities, with which he was ſo kind to furniſh me; and among the reſt, for an eſſay, of which he is himſelf the author, on the capacity and extent of the violoncello, in imitating the violin, flute, French horn, trumpet, hautboy, and baſſoon.

At Florence, I found the harpſichord of Zarlino, which is mentioned in the ſecond part of his Harmonical Inſtitutions, p. 140. This inſtrument was invented by Zarlino, in order to give the temperament and modulation of the three *genera*, the diatonic, chromatic, and enharmonic; and was conſtructed, under his direction, in the year 1548, by Dominico Peſareſe: it is now in the poſſeſſion of Signora Moncini, widow of the late compoſer Piſcetti. I copied Zarlino's inſtructions for tuning it, from his own hand-writing, on the back of the foreboard;

board; but I ſhall reſerve them, and the particular deſcription of this curious inſtrument, for the Hiſtory of Muſic, to which they more properly belong.

The grand duke's gallery, the Pitti palace, the Lorenziana, the Magliabecchi, and the Rinuccini libraries, all furniſhed reflections and materials for my intended work; and the converſations with which I was honoured by Dr. Bicchierai, Dr. Perelli, profeſſor of mathematics, Dr. Guadagni, profeſſor of experimental philoſophy, il propoſto Dr. Foſſi, Signor Bandini, librarian to the grand duke, and others; who facilitated my enquiries, and afforded me every opportunity for information I could wiſh, rendered by reſidence, in this delightful city, to which all the arts have been ſo much and ſo long indebted, at once both pleaſant and profitable.

S I E N N A.

There had been an opera, in this city, during the month of Auguſt, in which Signor

Signor Nicolini was the principal ſinger, and very much approved; but ſo capricious is public favour, that, with the ſame talents, the ſame voice, the ſame performers, and in the ſame compoſitions, he was totally diſliked and neglected, at Lucca, in the month of September!

MONTEFIASCONE.

September 18. In my way to Rome, I viſited Signor Guarducci, who has here built himſelf a very good houſe, and fitted it up in the Engliſh manner, with great taſte. He had already been apprized of my journey into Italy, and received me in the politeſt manner imaginable. He was ſo obliging as to let me hear him, in a ſong of Signor Sacchini's compoſition, which he ſung divinely. His voice, I think, is more powerful than when he was in England, and his taſte and expreſſion ſeem to have received every poſſible degree of ſelection and refinement. He is a very chaſte performer, and adds but

but few notes; thoſe few notes, however, are ſo well choſen, that they produce great effects, and leave the ear thoroughly ſatisfied. He has a winter-houſe in Florence, and has built this at Monteſiaſcone, the place of his birth, to retire to in ſummer, and to receive his mother, and his brothers and ſiſters: it is charmingly ſituated, commanding, on one ſide, a fine proſpect of the country, as far as Aquapendente, and a great part of the Lake of Bolſena; and, on the other, the hills of Viterbo, and the country leading to it. He ſays he has totally quitted the ſtage, and intends ſinging no more in public: this is a loſs to Italy, as I find he is now allowed by the Italians the firſt place among all the ſingers of the preſent period; and, at Rome, they ſtill ſpeak of his performance, in Piccini's *Didone Abbandonata*, with rapture. Signor Guarducci, in a manner truly obliging, gave me letters to eminent profeſſors at Rome and Naples, and not only treated me with the greateſt hoſpitality,

hoſpitality while under his roof, but loaded my chaiſe with exquiſite wine, the produce of his own vineyard, and with other refreſhments *.

R O M E.

It is impoſſible to approach this city, the capital of the world, for ſuch it *ſtill is* with reſpect to the arts, without ſenſations which no other ſituation can excite. The remains of antiquity, like the Sibyls works of old, become of greater value the leſs there is of them. At a traveller's firſt entrance into Rome, every ſtick, half devoured by time, or ſtone incruſted with moſs, is ſo intereſting, that his curioſity is not to be ſatisfied but by a moſt minute examination of it; leſt the precious fragments of ſome venerable pile, or the memorial of ſome illuſtrious atchievement, ſhould be paſſed unnoticed.

* The wine of Monteſiaſcone is proverbially famous all over Italy.

Though my views and expectations, on arriving in this city, were chiefly confined to antiquities, and the inedited materials with which the Vatican and other libraries might furnish me, relative to *ancient music*, yet I received great pleasure from the *modern*.

September 21. The day after my arrival, at his Grace the Duke of Dorset's, I heard Signor Celestini, the principal violin here, who is a very neat, and expressive performer: he was seconded by Signor Corri, who is an ingenious composer, and sings in a very good taste; there was likewise a good performer on the violoncello.

Signor Celestini played, among other things, one of his own solos, which was very pleasing, though extremely difficult, with great brilliancy, taste, and precision.

Saturday, Sept. 22. This evening Mr. Beckford, to whose zeal for the business in which I am embarked I have infinite obliga-

obligations, made a concert for me, consisting of twelve or fourteen of the best performers in Rome; these were led by Signor Celestini. There were three voices, Signor Cristofero, of the Pope's chapel, who sings very much in Guarducci's way, and is little inferior to him in delicacy; *il Grassetto*, a boy, who submitted to mutilation by his own choice, and against the advice of his friends, for the preservation of his voice, which is indeed a very good one, and he is, in other respects, a very pleasing singer; and a *buffo* tenor, a very comical fellow.

September 23. I was introduced to Signor Crispi, a celebrated *Maestro di Capella*, at whose house there was an *accademia* this evening, in which the vocal part was performed by his wife. This composer has an *accademia* at his house every Friday evening, at which there is usually a good band and much company.

September 24. There was a grand *Funzioni* at the *Santi Apostoli,* on account of the reconciliation of the Pope and the King of Portugal. It was at this church that I first saw his Holiness, and a great number of Cardinals, and heard *Te Deum.* There were two large bands of music, and an immense crowd. The music was composed by Signor Mosi. Cristofero sung charmingly; the airs were pretty, but the chorusses poor.

In the evening the outside of the cupola, church, and colonade of St. Peter, together with the Vatican palace, were finely illuminated, which affords a spectacle to the inhabitants of Rome, not to be equalled in the universe. And in the balconies, next to the street, at the palaces of most of the Cardinals, besides illuminations, there were concerts of very numerous bands of instrumental performers; but chiefly at the residence of the Portuguese Ambassador, where the hands employed amounted to above a hun-

hundred, and theſe continued their performance all night. However, this muſic, though in the open air, was too noiſy for me, and I retreated from it early, in order to have my ears ſoothed with more placid ſounds at the Duke of Dorſet's concert.

Tueſday 25. I had this morning the honour of being preſented to Cardinal Alexander Albani, principal librarian to the Vatican, and *Prefetto*, or Governor of the Pope's chapel. His eminence received me in the moſt obliging and condeſcending manner imaginable, taking me by the hand, and ſaying, *Figlio mio, che voleti?* "My ſon, what do you wiſh I "ſhould do for you?" And upon my telling the views with which I came into Italy, and expreſſing a deſire to be permitted to examine MSS. in the Vatican library, and in the archives of the pontifical chapel, relative to muſic, he ſaid, "You ſhall have the permiſſion you de-"ſire, but write it down in the form of "a memorial;" which being done, he called for his ſecretary, to whom he gave inſtructions to draw up an order, which he ſigned, and addreſſed to *Monſignore l'Arciveſcovo di Apomea, prefetto della Vacana*, to admit me into the Vatican library when I pleaſed, to let me ſee what books and MSS. I pleaſed, and to have copied what I pleaſed.

This was an important point gained, but, without the intelligence and aſſiſtance of the Abate Elie, one of the *cuſtodi*, or keepers of the books in the Vatican, I ſhould have been but little the better for the permiſſion I had obtained. For the MSS. in this celebrated library are ſo numerous, and many of them in ſuch diſorder, that to find the tracts I wiſhed would have been a work of years, had he not pointed them out *. This gentleman employed five or ſix whole days

* As yet there is no regular catalogue of the weſtern MSS. in the Vatican library. One was made and printed ſome years ago, in fourteen volumes

in making a catalogue for me of all that the Vatican contained relative to my work; after which I regularly ſpent my mornings there, in reading and marking ſuch things as I wiſhed to have copied entirely, or from which I was deſirous of extracts; and theſe my good friend the Abate undertook to tranſcribe for me, while I went to Naples.

During my firſt reſidence at Rome, I had ſo much to ſee, and ſo many enquiries to make, relative to ancient muſic, and ſpent ſo much time in the Vatican and other libraries, that I had but little to ſpare for the modern; however, that little was ſpent much to my ſatisfaction, in hearing public performances in the churches, and private concerts in the houſes of ſeveral profeſſors, as well as perſons of diſtinction. But as many days were ſpent here in much the ſame man-

lumes folio, of the eaſtern, but the author died before he had completed the work; and it has never ſince been reſumed by any other.

ner, to avoid repetition, I ſhall, for the preſent, drop the journal ſtile, and try to recollect the principal muſical events which happened while I was at Rome, without attending to dates; and, in enumerating theſe I ſhould think myſelf guilty of ingratitude, if I paſſed over in ſilence the countenance and aſſiſtance with which I was honoured by my own countrymen. I hope I ſhall therefore be pardoned the liberty of naming them occaſionally, with the reſpect due to their rank, and the ſervices I received from them.

And firſt, I cannot reſiſt the vanity of ſaying, that I paſſed few nights at Rome without hearing muſic at the Duke of Dorſet's; and that his grace had the goodneſs to contrive to have my curioſity gratified by ſomething new and curious, either in compoſition or performance, at moſt of theſe concerts. It was here that I had an opportunity of meeting the beſt performers in Rome, at a time when the theatres

theatres were ſhut, and it would have been difficult to have heard them elſe-where.

To Mr. Leighton, whoſe performance and taſte in muſic are ſuperior to thoſe of moſt gentlemen, I am indebted for ſome curious compoſitions, and for the converſation of ſeveral perſons in Rome, eminent for their ſkill in the art, and learning in the ſcience of ſound; among whom were the Marcheſe Gabriele, and Monſignor Reggio.

To the counſel and aſſiſtance of thoſe eminent antiquaries, Meſſieurs Jenkins, Morriſon, and Byers, I owe the greateſt part of my original drawings of ancient inſtruments; and to their active friendſhip I likewiſe owe much of the pleaſure and information I received at Rome.

And now, having acknowledged theſe debts to my countrymen, I muſt again ſay, that the men of learning and genius among the Italians have, throughout my journey, treated me with the utmoſt hoſ-

hoſpitality and kindneſs, each ſeeming to ſtrive who ſhould moſt contribute to my information and amuſement. For, except the civilities with which I was honoured at Venice and Florence by Mr. Richie, Sir Horace Mann, and Meſſieurs Perkins and Hempſon, I owe all my information and entertainment, till my arrival at Rome, to the Italians themſelves. Indeed, it was to them I chiefly addreſſed myſelf, thinking it moſt profitable, both in point of language and information, to mix with the natives. But at Rome and Naples I met with ſo many Engliſh, and found them all ſo ready to countenance and aſſiſt me in my enquiries, that I had no occaſion, or, indeed, time, to deliver ſeveral letters, with which I was furniſhed, to eminent perſons, in the literary and muſical world, at thoſe two capitals.

However, among the Romans I muſt diſtinguiſh *il Cavalier Pireneſe*, who gave me ſeveral drawings, and pointed out proper objects for others, of ſuch ancient inſtruments as ſtill ſubſiſt entire, among the beſt remains of antiquity; the Abate Orſini, a great collector of muſical compoſitions and tracts, who, among other uſeful materials for my intended work, furniſhed me with a ſight and catalogue of all the muſical dramas that have been performed at Rome, from the beginning of the laſt century to the preſent time; Counſellor Reiffenſtein, who, though not a native of Rome, has lived ſo long there, and is poſſeſſed of ſo much learning and taſte in the fine arts, that I found myſelf much enlightened by his converſation, and indebted to his zeal and intelligence for very ſingular ſervices; and the Cavalier Santarelli, *Capellano di Malta* *, and *Maeſtro di Capella* to his Holineſs.

To Signor Santarelli I was favoured with a letter from Padre Martini, which

* As Capellano di Malta he wears a ſmall croſs and an ivory ſtar on his breaſt.

had

had all the effect I could wiſh, as I ſoon found this excellent muſician and worthy man, not only diſpoſed to treat me with politeneſs, but even with friendſhip in the utmoſt extent of the word: he was the more able to render me real ſervices in my muſical enquiries, as, beſides his ſtation in the Pope's chapel, and his great ſkill and experience in the practical part, I found him deep in the theory, and learned in the hiſtory of his profeſſion, having been many years employed in the following curious work, *Della Muſica del Santuario e della diſciplina de ſuoi Cantori*; or, an Hiſtorical Diſſertation on Church Muſic. This work is divided into different centuries ſince the time of our Saviour, as *ſecolo primo*, *ſec. ſecundo*, *ſec. terzo*, &c. giving authorities throughout, from eccleſiaſtical hiſtory. The firſt volume was printed in the year 1764, but has never yet been publiſhed: the ſecond, in MS. is in great forwardneſs; it ſeems to ſupply all the deficiencies of another curious

curious and ſcarce work on the ſame ſubject, publiſhed in 1711, called *Oſſervazioni per ben regolare il coro della Capella pontificia*; or, Rules for conducting the Choir of the Pope's Chapel, by Andrea Adamo; but the hiſtorical part of this book, beginning only at the year 1400, and ending in 1711, that of Signor Santerelli, which begins with the earlieſt ages of the church, and continues to the preſent time, would certainly be a valuable acquiſition to ſuch lovers of church muſic as wiſh to trace it from it's ſource*.

* It ſeems as if Signor Santarelli was prevented from publiſhing his work, by the want of a patron worthy of it. He is ſo ſenſible of the contempt with which muſic is treated at preſent, by the firſt dignitaries of the church, that he entertains but ſmall hopes of the ſucceſs of his book, though it has been a work of much time and labour, and ſeems worthy the patronage and protection of his Holineſs, for the uſe of whoſe ſervants, as well as for the ſervice of muſic in general, it is in an eminent degree calculated.

Beſides

Besides communicating to me his unpublished printed book, and the second volume in MS. Signor Santarelli obliged me with extracts from two MS. volumes of curious anecdotes, and passages from old and scarce books relative to music; the whole collected in the course of many years conversation and reading. I must add to these favours, that of procuring me some of the most curious and scarce printed books which I sought at Rome: it was owing to his friendly zeal likewise, that, after three weeks spent in vain by myself and friends there, in search of the first *oratorio* that was ever set to music, I at length got a sight and copy of it; and, to crown the whole, he joined to all these benefits, not only that of furnishing me with a true and genuine copy of the famous *Miserere* of *Allegri*, but all the compositions performed in the Pope's chapel during Passion Week; together with many others of *Palestrina*, *Benevoli*, *Lucca Marenza*, and others which have never

been

been printed, nor have they ever been performed but in that chapel.

I was not more curious about the Vatican library, than the Pope's chapel, that celebrated ſanctuary in which church muſic ſeems to have had it's birth, or at leaſt to have received its firſt refinement; and concerning this chapel I was favoured with all the ſatisfaction I could wiſh from the Cav. Santarelli.

In the Pope's, or Siſtine chapel, no organ, or inſtrument of any kind, is employed in accompanying the voices, which conſiſt of thirty-two; eight baſes, eight tenors, eight counter-tenors, and eight ſopranos, or trebles; theſe are all in ordinary: there is likewiſe a number of ſupernumeraries ready to ſupply the places of thoſe who are occaſionally abſent, ſo that the ſingers are never fewer than thirty-two, on common days, but on great feſtivals they are nearly doubled*.

* Beſides the ſupernumerary *expectants* of this chapel, many of the capital opera ſingers from other

The dreſs of the ſingers in ordinary, is a kind of purple uniform; their pay is not great, and at preſent ſubjects of ſuperior merit, belonging to this eſtabliſhment, meet with but little notice or encouragement, ſo that muſic here begins to degenerate and decline very much; to which the high ſalaries given to fine voices and ſingers of great abilities in the numerous operas throughout Italy, and, indeed, all over Europe, greatly contribute, by little and little, all thoſe embelliſhments and refinements in the execution of ancient muſic, as well as the elegant ſimplicity for which that of this chapel is ſo celebrated, will be loſt. Formerly, even the *Canto Fermo* was here infinitely ſuperior to that of every other place by its purity, and by the expreſſive manner in which it was chanted.

I had indeed been told, before my arrival at Rome, by a friend who had re-

other parts of Italy, are employed in Paſſion Week.

ſided

ſided there nineteen years, that I muſt not expect to find the muſic of the Pope's chapel ſo ſuperior in the performance to that of the reſt of Italy, as it had been in times paſt, before operas were invented and ſuch great ſalaries given to the principal ſingers; *then* the Pope's muſicians being better paid, were conſequently more likely to be poſſeſſed of abilities ſuperior to thoſe elſewhere; but, at preſent, this is not the caſe, and the conſequence is obvious; their ſituation is ſomewhat ſimilar to that of our choriſters and choirmen in England, where their ſalaries remain at the original eſtabliſhment, and at that point of perfection their performance ſeems to remain likewiſe; living is dearer; money of leſs value; more is given elſewhere; another profeſſion is uſually tacked to that of ſinging, in order to obtain a livelihood; and church muſic, of courſe, falls into decay, and goes from bad to worſe, while that of the theatres receives daily improvements by additional rewards *.

* See remarks on Mr. Avifon's Effay on Mufical Expreffion, publifhed 1753, in which the author has well explained the caufes of degeneracy in our church mufic, and the want of fkill in the performers of it. With refpect to thefe he fays, "I believe "if the ftatutes of every cathedral were examined, "it would appear, that the falary allotted to each "member was exactly proportioned one to the other: "perhaps thus; to the chorifter, or finging boy, "five pounds; to the finging man, ten; to the "minor canon, twenty; the organift the fame; "to the canon or refidentiary, forty; and to the "dean, eighty pounds *per annum*; which, if mul-"tiplied by four, would make the firft twenty, the "fecond forty, the third eighty, the fourth one "hundred and fixty, and the fifth three hundred "and twenty: this, with the chance of livings to "the clergy, would be a decent competency for "each in his ftation; and I may venture to affirm, "that the three former would be very well con-"tented with it: yet, even this increafe will not "fatisfy the two latter; but, without fcruple or "remorfe, they (by what authority I know not) "divide three fourths of the profits arifing from "the portions allotted to their inferiors, among "themfelves; a manifeft abufe of the founder's in-"tention, and injuftice to the feveral incumbents: "hence a canonry comes to be valued at two hun-

"dred,

Signor Santarelli favoured me with the following particulars relative to the famous *Miſerere* of *Allegri* *. This piece, which, for upwards of a hundred and fifty years, has been annually performed in Paſſion Week at the Pope's chapel, on Wedneſday and Good-Friday, and which, in appearance, is ſo ſimple as to make thoſe, who have only ſeen it on paper, wonder whence its beauty and effect could ariſe, owes its reputation more to the manner in which it is performed, than to the compoſition: the ſame muſic is many times repeated to different words, and the ſingers have, by tradition, certain cuſtoms, expreſſions, and graces of convention, (*certe eſpreſſioni e Gruppi*) which produce

" dred, and a deanry at four hundred pounds *per* " *annum*; and if this computation over-rates the " value of ſome, others however muſt be allowed " to exceed it greatly."

* *Miſerere mei, Deus*, &c. Have mercy upon me, O God! pſ. 51. *Gregorio Allegri* was a deſcendant of the famous painter Correggio, whoſe family-name was *Allegri*.

great

great effects; such as swelling and diminishing the sounds altogether; accelerating or retarding the measure at some particular words, and singing some entire verses quicker than others. Thus far Signor Santarelli. Let me add, from *Andrea Adami*, in the work mentioned above, that, "After several vain attempts by "preceding composers, for more than a "hundred years, to set the same words "to the satisfaction of the heads of "the church; Gregorio Allegri succeed-"ed so well, as to merit eternal praise; "for with few notes, well modulated, "and well understood, he composed such "a *Miserere* as will continue to be sung "on the same days, every year, for ages "yet to come; and one that is conceived "in such just proportions as will asto-"nish future times, and ravish, as at pre-"sent, the soul of every hearer."

However, some of the great effects produced by this piece, may, perhaps, be justly attributed to the time, place, and solem-

nity

nity of the ceremonials, uſed during the performance: the pope and conclave are all proſtrated on the ground; the candles of the chapel, and the torches of the baluſtrade, are extinguiſhed, one by one; and the laſt verſe of this pſalm is terminated by two choirs; the *Maeſtro di Capella* beating time ſlower and ſlower, and the ſingers diminiſhing or rather *extinguiſhing* the harmony, by little and little, to a perfect point *.

It is likewiſe performed by ſelect voices, who have frequent rehearſals, particularly on the Monday in Paſſion Week, which is wholly ſpent in repeating and poliſhing the performance.

This compoſition uſed to be held ſo ſacred, that it was imagined excommunication would be the conſequence of an attempt to tranſcribe it. Padre Martini

* Adami's inſtructions are theſe:—*Averta pure il Signor Maeſtro che l'ultimo verſo del Salmo termina a due Cori, e però ſarà la Battuta Adagio, per finirlo Piano, ſmorzando a poco, a poco l'Armonia.*

Oſſerv. per reg. il Coro della cap. pont. p. 36.

told me there were never more than two copies of it made by authority, one of which was for the late king of Portugal, and the other for himſelf: this laſt he permitted me to tranſcribe at Bologna, and Signor Santarelli favoured me with another copy from the archives of the Pope's chapel: upon collating theſe two copies, I find them to agree pretty exactly, except in the firſt verſe. I have ſeen ſeveral ſpurious copies of this compoſition in the poſſeſſion of different perſons, in which the melody of the *ſoprano*, or upper part, was tolerably correct, but the other parts differed very much; and this inclined me to ſuppoſe the upper part to have been written from memory, which, being ſo often repeated to different words in the performance, would not be difficult to do, and the other parts to have been made to it by ſome modern contra-puntiſt afterwards.

Before I quit a ſubject ſo intereſting to the lovers of church muſic, I ſhall add the

the following anecdote, which was given me likewiſe by Signor Santarelli.

The Emperor Leopold the firſt, not only a lover and patron of muſic, but a good compoſer himſelf, ordered his ambaſſador, at Rome, to entreat the Pope to permit him to have a copy of the celebrated *Miſerere* of *Allegri*, for the uſe of the Imperial chapel at Vienna; which being granted, a copy was made by the *Signor Maeſtro* of the Pope's chapel, and ſent to the Emperor, who had then in his ſervice ſome of the firſt ſingers of the age; but, notwithſtanding the abilities of the performers, this compoſition was ſo far from anſwering the expectations of the Emperor and his court, in the execution, that he concluded the Pope's *Maeſtro di Capella*, in order to keep it a myſtery, had put a trick upon him, and ſent him another compoſition *. Upon which, in

* Signor Santarelli's words were theſe :—*Quantunque Cantato da Muſici ſoaviſſimi, fece alla Corte di Vienna la Miſera Comparſa di un ſempliciſſimo falſo Bordone.*

great wrath, he ſent an expreſs to his Holineſs, with a complaint againſt the *Maeſtro di Capella,* which occaſioned his immediate diſgrace, and diſmiſſion from the ſervice of the papal chapel; and in ſo great a degree was the Pope offended, at the ſuppoſed impoſition of his compoſer, that, for a long time, he would neither ſee him, or hear his defence; however, at length, the poor man got one of the cardinals to plead his cauſe, and to acquaint his Holineſs, that the ſtile of ſinging in his chapel, particularly in performing the *Miſerere,* was ſuch as could not be expreſſed by notes, nor taught or tranſmitted to any other place, but by example; for which reaſon the piece in queſtion, though faithfully tranſcribed, muſt fail in its effect, when performed elſewhere. His Holineſs did not underſtand muſic, and could hardly comprehend how the ſame notes ſhould ſound ſo differently in different places; however, he ordered his *Maeſtro di Capella* to write down his defence,

defence, in order to be ſent to Vienna, which was done; and the Emperor, ſeeing no other way of gratifying his wiſhes with reſpect to this compoſition, begged of the Pope, that ſome of the muſicians in the ſervice of his Holineſs, might be ſent to Vienna, to inſtruct thoſe in the ſervice of his chapel how to perform the *Miſerere* of Allegri, in the ſame expreſſive manner as in the Siſtine chapel at Rome, which was granted. But, before they arrived, a war broke out with the Turks, which called the emperor from Vienna; and the *Miſerere* has never yet, perhaps, been truly performed, but in the Pope's chapel.

I viſited ſeveral times, while I was at Rome, Signor Mazzanti, who not only ſings with exquiſite taſte, but is likewiſe an excellent muſician. He is both a reader and a writer on the ſubject of muſic, as well as a conſiderable collector of books and manuſcripts. The richneſs

of

of his taſte, in ſinging, makes ample a-mends for the want of force in his voice, which is now but a thread. He has a great collection of Paleſtrini's compoſitions, and furniſhed me with ſeveral of them, which I could not get elſewhere. Signor Mazzanti is famous for ſinging the poem of Taſſo to the ſame melody as the Barcarolles of Venice. This he does with infinite taſte, accompanying himſelf on the violin, with the harmony of which he produces curious and pleaſing effects. I prevailed on him to write me down the original melody, in order to compare it with one that I took down at Venice, while it was ſinging on the great canal. He has compoſed many things himſelf, ſuch as operas and motets for voices; and trios, quartets, quintets, and other pieces for violins. He plays pretty well on the violin, and is in poſſeſſion of the moſt beautiful and perfect *Steiner* I ever ſaw. He has advanced very far in the theory of

muſic;

muſic; has made, by way of ſtudy, an abridgment of the modulation of Paleſtrini, which is well ſelected and digeſted; and he ſhewed me a conſiderable part of a muſical treatiſe, in manuſcript, written by himſelf.

At Rome I alſo had frequent converſations with Rinaldo di Capua, an old and excellent Neapolitan compoſer. He is the natural ſon of a perſon of very high rank in that country, and at firſt only ſtudied muſic as an accompliſhment; but being left by his father with only a ſmall fortune, which was ſoon diſſipated, he was forced to make it his profeſſion. He was but ſeventeen when he compoſed his firſt opera at Vienna. I have often received great pleaſure from his compoſitions; he is not in great faſhion at preſent, though he compoſed an *intermezzo* for the *Capranica* theatre at Rome, laſt winter, which had great ſucceſs. He is very intelligent in converſation; but, though a good-

good-natured man, his opinions are rather ſingular and ſevere upon his brother compoſers. He thinks they have nothing left to do now, but to write themſelves and others over again; and that the only chance they have left for obtaining the reputation of novelty and invention, ariſes either from ignorance or want of memory in the public; as every thing, both in melody and modulation, that is worth doing, has been often already done. He includes himſelf in the cenſure; and frankly confeſſes, that though he has written full as much as his neighbours, yet out of all his works, perhaps not above *one* new melody can be found, which has been wire-drawn in different keys, and different meaſures, a thouſand times. And as to modulation, it muſt be always the ſame, to be natural and pleaſing; what has not been given to the public being only the refuſe of thouſands, who have tried and rejected it, either

either as impracticable or displeasing. The only opportunity a composer has for introducing new modulation in songs, is in a short second part, in order to *fright* the hearer back to the first, to which it serves as a foil, by making it comparitively beautiful. He likewise censures with great severity the noise and tumult of instruments in modern songs.

Signor Rinaldo di Capua has at Rome the reputation of being the inventor of accompanied recitatives; but in hunting for old compositions in the archives of S. Gerolamo della Carità, I found an oratorio by Alessandro Scarlatti, which was composed in the latter end of the last century, before Rinaldo di Capua was born, and in which are *accompanied recitatives*. But he does not himself pretend to the invention; all he claims is the being among the first who introduced long *ritornellos*, or symphonies, into the recitatives of strong passion and distress,

which

which expreſs or imitate what it would be ridiculous for the voice to attempt. There are many fine ſcenes of this kind in his works, and Haſſe, Galuppi, Jomelli, and Piccini have been very happy in ſuch intereſting, and often ſublime compoſitions.

In the courſe of a long life Rinaldo di Capua has experienced various viciſſitudes of fortune; ſometimes in vogue, ſometimes neglected. However, when he found old age coming on, he collected together his principal works, ſuch as had been produced in the zenith of his fortune and fancy; thinking theſe would be a reſource in diſtreſsful times. Theſe times came; various misfortunes and calamities befel him and his family, when, behold, this reſource, this ſole reſource, the accumulated produce of his pen, had, by a graceleſs ſon been ſold for waſte paper!

The Roman performers from whom I received the greateſt pleaſure, were, in the vocal, Signor Criſtofero, of the Pope's chapel, for voice and high finiſhing; Signor Mazzanti for taſte and knowledge of muſic; La Bacchelli, commonly called the *Mignatrice* *, for brilliancy and variety of ſtile; and the eldeſt daughter of the celebrated painter Cavalier Battoni, a *dilettante*, and ſcholar of Signor Santarelli, for art where no art appears, and for that elegant ſimplicity, and truly pathetic expreſſion, which cannot be defined.

The beſt violin performers were, Signor Celeſtini, whom I before mentioned; Signor Niccolai, a worthy ſcholar of Tartini; and Signor Ruma, a young man whom I frequently heard at Signor Criſpi's concerts, who plays with great facility and neatneſs.

* Her profeſſion is not muſic, but painting in miniature.

The

The Abate Roſſi is reckoned the neateſt harpſichord player at Rome; and Signor Criſpi, without pretenſion, is a good performer on that inſtrument. But, to ſay the truth, I have neither met with a *great* player on the harpſichord, nor an *original* compoſer for it throughout Italy*. There is no accounting for this but by the little uſe which is made of that inſtrument there, except to accompany the voice. It is at preſent ſo much neglected both by the maker and player, that it is difficult to ſay whether the inſtruments themſelves, or the performers are the worſt †.

* It ſeems as if Alberti was always to be pillaged or imitated in every modern harpſichord leſſon.

† To perſons accuſtomed to Engliſh harpſichords, all the keyed inſtruments on the continent appear to great diſadvantage. Throughout Italy they have generally little octave ſpinets to accompany ſinging, in private houſes, ſometimes in a triangular form, but more frequently in the ſhape of our old virginals; of which the keys are ſo noiſy, and the tone ſo feeble, that more wood is heard than wire. The beſt Italian harpſichord I met with

But with regard to the organ, I have frequently heard it judiciously and spiritedly played in Italy. At Milan, San Martini has a way peculiar to himself of touching that instrument, which is truly masterly and pleasing. The first organists of St. Marc's church at Venice, of the Duomo at Florence, and of St. John Lateran at Rome (of whom I shall have occasion to speak hereafter) are very superiour in their performance to most others I have heard on the continent. But, in general, the best organists in Italy are the monks and friars, many of whom I have heard play in the churches

for touch, was that of Signor Grimani at Venice; and for tone, that of Monsignor Reggio at Rome; but I found three English harpsichords in the three principal cities of Italy, which are regarded by the Italians as so many phenomena. One was made by Shudi, and is in the possession of the Hon. Mrs. Hamilton at Naples. The other two, which are of Kirkman's make, belong to Mrs. Richie at Venice, and to the Hon. Mrs. Earl, who resided at Rome when I was there.

and chapels of their own convents, not only in a maſterly, but a brilliant and modern manner, without forgetting the genius of the inſtrument. And ſome of the girls of the Venetian Conſervatorios, as well as the nuns in different parts of Italy, play with rapidity and neatneſs in their ſeveral churches; but there is almoſt always a want of force, of learning, and courage in female performances, occaſioned, perhaps, by that feminine ſoftneſs, with which, in other ſituations, we are ſo enchanted.

Having heard the moſt eminent performers; converſed with the principal theoriſt and compoſers, found many of the books manuſcripts, and antiquities I had ſought and explained my wants with regard to the reſt, to ſeveral friends at Rome, who kindly promiſed me their aſſiſtance in ſupplying them during my abſence; I ſet off for Naples on Sunday evening, the fourteenth of October.

NAPLES

NAPLES.

I entered this city, impreſſed with the higheſt ideas of the perfect ſtate in which I ſhould find practical muſic. It was at Naples only that I expected to have my ears gratified with every muſical luxury and refinement which Italy could afford. My viſits to other places were in the way of *buſineſs*, for the performance of a *taſk* I had aſſigned myſelf; but I came hither animated by the hope of pleaſure. And what lover of muſic could be in the place which had produced the two Scarlattis, Vinci, Leo, Pergoleſe, Porpora, Farinelli, Jomelli, Piccini, and innumerable others of the firſt eminence among compoſers and performers, both vocal and inſtrumental, without the moſt ſanguine expectations. How far theſe expectations were gratified, the Reader will find in the courſe of my narrative, which is conſtantly a faithful tranſcript of my feelings at the time I entered them in my journal, immediately after hearing and ſeeing, with a mind not conſcious of any prejudice or partiality.

I arrived here about five o'clock in the evening, on Tueſday, October 16, and at night went to the *Teatro de' Fiorentini*, to hear the comic opera of *Geloſia per Geloſia,* ſet to muſic by Signor Piccini. This theatre is as ſmall as Mr. Foote's in London, but higher, as there are five rows of boxes in it. Notwithſtanding the court was at Portici, and a great number of families at their *Villeggiature*, or country-houſes, ſo great is the reputation of Signor Piccini, that every part of the houſe was crowded. Indeed this opera had nothing elſe but the merit and reputation of the compoſer to ſupport it, as both the drama and ſinging were bad. There was, however, a comic character performed by Signor Caſaccia, a man of infinite humour; the whole houſe was in a roar the inſtant he appeared; and the pleaſantry of this actor did not conſiſt

ſiſt in buffoonery, nor was it local, which in Italy, and, indeed, elſewhere, is often the caſe; but was of that original and general ſort as would excite laughter at all times and in all places.

The airs of this burletta are full of pretty paſſages, and, in general, moſt ingeniouſly accompanied: there was no dancing, ſo that the acts, of which there were three, ſeemed rather long.

There are three Conſervatorios in this city, for the education of *boys* who are intended for the profeſſion of muſic, of the ſame kind with thoſe of Venice, for *girls*. As the ſcholars in the Venetian Conſervatorios have been juſtly celebrated for their taſte and neatneſs of execution, ſo thoſe of Naples have long enjoyed the reputation of being the firſt *contra-puntiſts* or compoſers in Europe.

Wedneſday 17. This afternoon I went to hear a muſical performance at the church of the Franciſcans, where the three Conſervatorios were to furniſh mufic and muficians for a great feftival of eight fucceffive days, morning and evening*. This is a large handfome church, but too much ornamented. The architecture feems to be good, but it is fo be-gilt that it almoft blinded me to look at it; and in the few interftitial parts where there is no gold, tawdry flowers are painted in abundance.

The band was numerous, confifting of above a hundred voices and inftruments. They were placed in a long occafional gallery, totally covered with gold and filver gilding; but though the band feemed to be a very good one, and the leader very careful and attentive, yet the diftance of fome of the performers from the others, rendered it almoft impoffible that the time fhould be always exactly kept.

* It is by this performance that the Confervatorios hold their charters; and, in confideration of the boys playing gratis, they are exempted by the King from all taxes upon wine and provifions, which are paid by the other inhabitants of Naples.

The

The compoſition was by Signor Gennaro Manni, and in many movements admirable; he attended himſelf to beat the time. The opening was in a rough ſtile; after which this ſpecies of overture was made an accompaniment to a chorus, which was well written. Several airs and a duet ſucceeded, which pleaſed me extremely; there were fancy and contrivance; light and ſhade; and though the ſinging was not of the firſt claſs, yet there was a counter-tenor and a baſe which I liked very much. The counter-tenor had one of the moſt powerful voices I ever heard; he made his way through the whole band, in the loudeſt and moſt tumultuous parts of the choruſſes. When he had an air to ſing alone, his ſhake was good, and his ſtile plain, but his *portamento* was a little deficient, and rather ſavoured of what we call in England the cathedral manner of ſinging, through the throat. The air which was given to the baſe was as ingeniouſly written as any I ever heard; the accompaniments were full, without deſtroying the melody of the voice parts: inſtead of ſhortening or mutilating its paſſages, the inſtruments ſeemed to continue and finiſh them, giving the ſinger time for reſpiration. In a duet between two *ſopranos*, the accompaniments were likewiſe admirable; as they were in a chorus which had many ſolo parts in it. After this the author did not ſeem to be ſo happy. There were ſome trifling, and ſome heavy movements; in the former of which there was no other novelty than that of throwing the accent upon the wrong note; for inſtance, upon the ſecond inſtead of the firſt; or, in common time, upon the fourth inſtead of the third. This may have its merit in comic operas, where ſome humour is ſeconded by it, but ſurely ſuch a poor expedient is beneath the dignity of church muſic, where a grave and majeſtic ſtile ſhould be preſerved, even in rapid movements. But the ſame rage for novelty, which

which has occaſioned ſuch ſudden revolutions in the muſic of Italy, gives birth, ſometimes, to ſtrange *concetti.*

The national muſic here is ſo ſingular, as to be totally different, both in melody and modulation, from all I have heard elſewhere. This evening in the ſtreets there were two people ſinging alternately; one of theſe Neapolitan *Canzoni* was accompanied by a violin and *calaſcione* *. The ſinging is noiſy and vulgar, but the accompaniments are admirable, and well performed. The violin and calaſcione parts were inceſſantly at work during the ſong, as well as the ritornels. The modulation ſurpriſed me very much: from the key of A natural, to that of C and F, was not difficult or new; but from that of A, with a ſharp third, to E flat, was aſtoniſhing;

* The Calaſcione is an inſtrument very common at Naples; it is a ſpecies of guitar, with only two ſtrings, which are tuned fifths to each other.

and

and the more ſo, as the return to the orginal key was always ſo inſenſibly managed, as neither to ſhock the ear, nor to be eaſily diſcovered by what road or relations it was brought about.

Thurſday 18. I was very happy to find, upon my arrival at Naples, that though many perſons to whom I had letters, were in the country, yet Signor Jomelli and Signor Piccini were in town. Jomelli was preparing a ſerious opera for the great theatre of S. Carlo, and Piccini had juſt brought the burletta on the ſtage which I have mentioned before.

This morning I viſited Signor Piccini, and had the pleaſure of a long converſation with him. He ſeems to live in a reputable way, has a good houſe, and many ſervants and attendants about him. He is not more than four or five and forty; looks well, has a very animated countenance, and is a polite and agreeable little man, though rather grave in his manner for a Neapolitan poſſeſſed of ſo

much

much fire and genius. His family is rather numerous; one of his sons is a student in the university of Padua. After reading a letter which Mr. Giardini was so obliging as to give me to him, he told me he should be extremely glad if he could be of any use either to me or my work. My first enquiries were concerning the Neapolitan Conservatorios; for he having been brought up in one of them himself, his information was likely to be authentic and satisfactory. In my first visit I confined my questions chiefly to the four following subjects:

1. The antiquity of these establishments.

2. Their names.

3. The number of masters and scholars.

4. The time for admission, and for quitting these schools.

To my first demand he answered, that the Conservatorios were of ancient standing, as might be seen by the ruinous condition

dition of one of the buildings, which was ready to tumble down *.

To my ſecond, that their names were *S. Onofrio*, *La Pietà*, and *Santa Maria di Loreto*.

To my third queſtion he anſwered, that the number of ſcholars in the firſt Conſervatorio is about ninety, in the ſecond a hundred and twenty, and in the other, two hundred.

That each of them has two principal *Maeſtri di Capella*, the firſt of whom ſuperintends and correcťs the compoſitions of the ſtudents; the ſecond the ſinging, and gives leſſons. That there are aſſiſtant maſters, who are called *Maeſtri Secolari*; one for the violin, one for the violoncello, one for the harpſichord, one for the hautbois, one for the French horn, and ſo for other inſtruments.

* I afterwards obtained, from good authority, the exact date of each of theſe foundations; their fixed and ſtated rules, amounting to thirty-one; and the orders given to the Rectors for regulating the conduct and ſtudies of the boys, every month in the year.

To

To my fourth enquiry he anſwered, that boys are admitted from eight or ten to twenty years of age; that when they are taken in young they are bound for eight years; but, when more advanced, their admiſſion is difficult, except they have made a conſiderable progreſs in the ſtudy and practice of muſic. That after boys have been in a Conſervatorio for ſome years, if no genius is diſcovered, they are diſmiſſed to make way for others. That ſome are taken in as penſioners, who pay for their teaching; and others, after having ſerved their time out, are retained to teach the reſt; but that in both theſe caſes they are allowed to go out of the Conſervatorio at pleaſure.

I enquired throughout Italy at what place boys were chiefly qualified for ſinging by caſtration, but could get no certain intelligence. I was told at Milan that it was at Venice; at Venice, that it was at Bologna; but at Bologna the fact was denied, and I was referred to Flo-

rence;

rence; from Florence to Rome, and from Rome I was sent to Naples. The operation most certainly is against law in all these places, as well as against nature; and all the Italians are so much ashamed of it, that in every province they transfer it to some other.

> "Ask where's the North? at York, 'tis on the Tweed;
> "In Scotland, at the Orcades; and there,
> "At Greenland, Zembla, or the Lord knows where." *Pope's Ess. on Man.*

However, with respect to the Conservatorios at Naples, Mr. Gemineau, the British consul, who has so long resided there, and who has made very particular enquiries, assured me, and his account was confirmed by Dr. Cirillo, an eminent and learned Neapolitan physician, that this practice is absolutely forbiden in the Conservatorios, and that the young *Castrati* came from Leccia in Apuglia; but, before the operation is performed, they are brought to a Conservatorio to be tried as to the probability of voice, and then

then are taken home by their parents for this barbarous purpoſe. It is, however, death by the laws to all thoſe who perform the operation, and excommunication to every one concerned in it, unleſs it be done, as is often pretended, upon account of ſome diſorders which may be ſuppoſed to require it, and with the conſent of the boy. And there are inſtances of its being done even at the requeſt of the boy himſelf, as was the caſe of the Graſſetto at Rome. But as to theſe previous trials of the voice, it is my opinion that the cruel operation is but too frequently performed without trial, or at leaſt without ſufficient proofs of an improvable voice; otherwiſe ſuch numbers could never be found in every great town throughout Italy, without any voice at all, or at leaſt without one ſufficient to compenſate ſuch a loſs. Indeed all the *muſici** in the churches at

* The word *muſico*, in Italy, ſeems now wholly appropriated to a ſinger with a *ſoprano* or *contr' alto* voice, which has been preſerved by art.

pre-

present are made up of the refuse of the opera houses, and it is very rare to meet with a tolerable voice upon the establishment in any church throughout Italy. The *virtuosi* who sing there occasionally, upon great festivals only, are usually strangers, and paid by the time.

I went again this afternoon to the Franciscan's church, where there was a larger band than the day before. The whole Conservatorio of the Pietà, consisting of a hundred and twenty boys, all dressed in a blue uniform, attended. The *Sinfonia* was just begun when I arrived; it was very brilliant, and well executed: then followed a pretty good chorus; after which, an air by a tenor voice, one by a *soprano*, one by a *contr' alto*, and another by a different tenor; but worse singing I never heard before, in Italy; all was unfinished and *scholar-like*; the closes stiff, studied, and ill executed; and nothing like a shake could be mustered out of the whole band of singers. The *soprano* forced the

the high notes in a falſe direction, till they penetrated the brain of every hearer; and the baſe ſinger was as rough as a maſtiff, whoſe barking he ſeemed to imitate. A young man played a ſolo concerto on the baſſoon, in the ſame incorrect and unmaſterly manner, which drove me out of the church before the veſpers were finiſhed.

From hence I went directly to the comic opera, which, to-night, was at the *Teatro Nuova*. This houſe is not only leſs than the *Fiorentini*, but is older and more dirty. The way to it, for carriages, is through ſtreets very narrow, and extremely inconvenient. This burletta was called *Le Trame per Amore*, and ſet by Signor Giovanni Paeſiello, *Maeſtro di Capella Napolitano*. The ſinging was but indifferent; there were nine characters in the piece, and yet not one good voice among them; however, the muſic pleaſed me very much; it was full of fire and fancy, the ritornels abounding in new paſſages, and the vocal parts in elegant and ſimple melodies, ſuch as might be remembered and carried away after the firſt hearing, or be performed in private by a ſmall band, or even without any other inſtrument than a harpſichord *. The overture, of one movement only, was quite comic, and contained a perpetual ſucceſſion of pleaſant paſſages. There was no dancing, which made it neceſſary to ſpin the acts out to rather a tireſome length. The airs were much applauded, though it was the fourteenth repreſentation of the opera. The author was engaged to compoſe for Turin, at the

* This is ſeldom the caſe in modern opera ſongs, ſo crowded is the ſcore and the orcheſtra. Indeed Piccini is accuſed of employing inſtruments to ſuch exceſs, that in Italy no copyiſt will tranſcribe one of his operas without being paid a zechin more than for one by any other compoſer. But in burlettas he has generally bad voices to write for, and is obliged to produce all his effects with inſtruments; and, indeed, this kind of drama uſually abounds with brawls and *ſquabbles*, which it is neceſſary to enforce with the orcheſtra.

next

next carnival, for which place he ſet out while I was at Naples. The performance began about a quarter before eight, and continued till paſt eleven o'clock.

Friday 19. This evening I went a third time to St. Franceſco's church, and heard the performance of the ſcholars of another Conſervatorio, Santa Mara di Loreto. They appeared all in a white uniform, with a black kind of ſaſh. The ſinging was a little better than the day before, but the inſtruments were hardly ſo good. The firſt air, after a ſpirited overture and chorus, was ſung by an inoffenſive tenor; then another air by a ſoprano, not quite ſo; after which, a third air by a baſe voice, the direct contrary of inoffenſive. Such a bawling Stentor, with a throat ſo inflexible, ſure never exiſted before. The diviſions were ſo rough and ſo ſtrongly marked, that they became quite groteſque and ridiculous; if it had not been for the ſerious effect which his performance had on the melancholy audience, no one could poſſibly have ſuppoſed it to be ſerious. A ſolo on the coarſeſt double baſe that was ever played upon, would have been melifluous, by compariſon. After him, a middling counter-tenor ſung, which even ſo ſtrong a foil could not make agreeable; and then another ſoprano, not at all a hopeleſs ſubject: his voice was well toned, and he had a little improvable ſhake. In ſhort, this was the only promiſing ſinger I had heard for two days. But to the bad voices, ſo ſlovenly, ignorant, and unfiniſhed a manner was added, that the people were ſung out of church as faſt as they came in. There was a young man who played ſolo parts in the ritornels with a kind of clarinet, which they call at Naples a *vox humana*; another on the trumpet, and a third on the hautbois; but in an incorrect and unintereſting manner. The boys who ſung had very poor cadences to their ſongs, which,

which, as they uſually had ſecond parts, were always repeated after the *da capo*.

Saturday, 20. This morning I heard, at the ſame church, the boys of the Conſervatorio of *St. Onofrio*, who wear a white uniform. The performance was much the ſame as that of the other two. Theſe ſeminaries, which have heretofore produced ſuch great profeſſors, ſeem at preſent to be but low in genius. However, ſince theſe inſtitutions, as well as others, are ſubject to fluctuations, after being languid for ſome time, like their neighbour Mount Veſuvius, they will, perhaps, blaze out again with new vigour.

Sunday 21, and *Monday* 22. were ſpent in viſiting the environs of Naples. However, I arrived in town ſoon enough on Monday night to hear Paeſiello's opera, a ſecond time, at the *Teatro Nuovo*. It pleaſed me full as much now as before, and in the ſame places. The overture ſtill ſeemed comic and original, the airs far from common, though in general plain and ſimple. If this compoſer has any fault, it is in repeating paſſages too often, even to five or ſix times, which is like driving a nail into a plaiſtered wall; two or three ſtrokes fix it better than more, for after that number, it either grows looſe, or recoils: thus an energy is often given by reiterated ſtrokes on the tympanum; but too often repeated, they not only ceaſe to make any further impreſſion, but ſeem to obliterate thoſe already made. I ſtill think this opera too long for want of the *intermezzi* of dancing *.

Tueſday 23. This evening hearing in the ſtreet ſome genuine Neapolitan ſinging, accompanied by a calaſcioncina, a mandoline, and a violin; I ſent for the whole band up ſtairs, but, like other ſtreet muſic, it was beſt at a diſtance; in the room it was coarſe, out of tune, and out of harmony; whereas, in the ſtreet,

* I was afterwards informed that dancing is not allowed in any other theatre at Naples than that of St. Carlo, which is the theatre royal.

it ſeemed the contrary of all this: however, let it be heard where it will, the modulation and accompaniment are very extraordinary.

In the canzone of to-night they began in A natural, and, without well knowing how, they got into the moſt extraneous keys it is poſſible to imagine, yet without offending the ear. After the inſtruments have played a long ſymphony in A, the ſinger begins in F, and ſtops in C, which is not uncommon or difficult; but, after another ritornel, from F, he gets into E flat, then cloſes in A natural; after this there were tranſitions even into B flat, and D flat, without given offence, returning, or rather *ſliding*; always into the original key of A natural, the inſtruments moving the whole time in quick notes, without the leaſt intermiſſion. The voice part is very ſlow, a kind of pſalmody; the words, of which there are many ſtanzas to the ſame air, are in the Neapolitan language, which is as different from good Italian, as Welſh from Engliſh. It is a very ſingular ſpecies of muſic, as wild in modulation, and as different from that of all the reſt of Europe as the Scots, and is, perhaps, as ancient, being among the common people merely traditional. However, the violin player wrote down the melody of the voice part for me, and afterwards brought me ſomething like the accompaniment; but theſe parts have a ſtrange appearance when ſeen on paper together. I heard theſe muſicians play a great number of Neapolitan airs, but all were different from other muſic.

A little before Chriſtmas, muſicians of this ſort come from Calabria to Naples, and *their* muſic is wholly different from this; they uſually ſing with a guitar and violin, not on the ſhoulder, but hanging down. Paeſiello had introduced ſome of this muſic into his comic opera, which was now in run. Signor Piccini promiſed to procure me ſome of theſe

these wild national melodies. Another sort is peculiar to Apuglia, with which the people are set a-dancing and sweating, who either have, or would be thought to have been bitten by the tarantula. Of this music Dr. Cirillo procured me a specimen. Signor Serrao, in a dissertation on the subject, and Dr. Cirillo, who has made several experiments, in order to determine the fact, are both of opinion that the whole is an imposition, practised by the people of Apuglia, to gain money: that not only the cure but the malady itself is a fraud. Dr. Cirillo assured me that he had never been able to provoke the tarantula either to bite himself or others upon whom he had repeatedly tried the experiment *. However, the whole is so throughly believed by some inocent people in the country,

* This account may perhaps diminish the honour of music, by augmenting the number of sceptics, as to its *miraculous powers*; yet truth requires it should be given.

that, when really bitten by other insects or animals that are poisonous, they take this method of dancing, to a particular tune, till they sweat; which, together with their faith, sometimes makes them whole. They will continue the dance, in a kind of frenzy, for many hours, even till they drop down with fatigue and lassitude.

Wednesday 24. I went again this evening to Piccini's opera, but was too late for the overture; the house was very full, and the music pleased me more than the first time. The airs are not so familiar as those in Paesiello's opera, yet there is much better writing in them; and there are some accompanied recitatives, in the ritornels of which, though several different parts are going on at the same time, there is a clearness, and, if it may be so called, a *transparency*, which is wondeful. The singing, as I before observed, is wretched; but there is so much *vis comica* in Casaccia, that his singing is never thought

thought of; yet, for want of dancing, the acts are neceſſarily ſo long, that it is wholly impoſſible to keep up the attention; ſo that thoſe who are not talking, or playing at cards, uſually fall aſleep.

Thurſday 25. After dinner I went once more to hear the boys of St. Onofrio, at the Franciſcans church. They performed a Litany, that was compoſed by Durante*; the reſt of the muſic, which ſeemed to be that of a raw and inexperienced compoſer, was by a young man, who beat time. There was again a ſolo on the inſtrument called *la Voce Hu-*

* Durante, who has been dead ſome years, was a long time Maſter to the Conſervatorio of St. Onofrio. From the character Mr. Rouſſeau has given of this compoſer, I had conceived the higheſt ideas of his merit; and in the courſe of my journey through Italy, I collected a great number of his compoſitions for the church. M. Rouſſeau's words in ſpeaking of him are very ſtrong: "*Durante eſt le plus grand harmoniſte de l'Italie, c'eſt à dire du monde,*" Dict. de Muſique.

mana;

mana; it is of an agreeable tone, has a great compaſs, but was not well played on. A concerto on the violin was likewiſe introduced, where hand and fire were diſcovered by the player, but no taſte or finiſhing.

Friday 26. This morning I firſt had the pleaſure of ſeeing and converſing with Signor Jomelli, who arrived at Naples from the country but the night before. He is extremely corpulent, and, in the face, not unlike what I remember Handel to have been, yet far more polite and ſoft in his manner. I found him in his night-gown, at an inſtrument, writing. He received me very politely, and made many apologies for not having called on me, in conſequence of a card I had left at his houſe; but apologies were indeed unneceſſary, as he was but juſt come to town, and at the point of bringing out a new opera, that muſt have occupied both his time and thoughts ſufficiently. He had heard of me from Mr. Hamilton. I gave him

him Padre Martini's letter, and after he had read it we went to buſineſs directly. I told him my errand to Italy, and ſhewed him my plan, for I knew his time was precious. He read it with great attention, and converſed very openly and rationally; ſaid the part I had undertaken was much neglected at preſent in Italy; that the Conſervatorios, of which, I told him, I wiſhed for information, were now at a low ebb, though formerly ſo fruitful in great men. He mentioned to me a perſon of great learning, who had been tranſlating David's Pſalms into excellent Italian verſe; in the courſe of which work, he had found it neceſſary to write a diſſertation on the muſic of the ancients, which he had communicated to him. He ſaid this writer was a fine and ſubtle critic; had differed in ſeveral points from Padre Martini; had been in correſpondence with Metaſtaſio, and had received a long letter from him on the ſubject of lyric poetry and muſic; all which he thought

thought neceſſary for me to ſee. He promiſed to procure me the book, and to make me acquainted with the author. He ſpoke very much in praiſe of Aleſſandro Scarlatti, as to his church muſic, ſuch as motets, maſſes, and oratorios; promiſed to procure me information concerning the Conſervatorios, and whatever elſe was to my purpoſe, and in his power. He took down my direction, and aſſured me that the inſtant he had got his opera on the ſtage, he ſhould be entirely at my ſervice. Upon my telling him that my time for remaining at Naples was very ſhort, that I ſhould even then have been on the road in my way home, but for his opera, which I ſo much wiſhed to hear; that beſides urgent buſineſs in England, there was great probability of a war, which would keep me a priſoner on the continent: he, in anſwer to that, and with great appearance of ſincerity, ſaid, if after I returned to England, any thing of importance to my plan occured, he he would not fail of ſending it to me. In ſhort, I went away in high good humour with this truly great compoſer, who is indiſputably one of the firſt of his profeſſion now alive in the univerſe; for were I to name the living compoſers of Italy for the ſtage, according to my idea of their merit, it would be in the following order: Jomelli, Galuppi, Piccini, and Sacchini. It is, however, difficult to decide which of the two compoſers firſt-mentioned, has merited moſt from the public; Jomelli's works are full of great and noble ideas, treated with taſte and learning; Galuppi's abound in fancy, fire, and feeling; Piccini has far ſurpaſſed all his cotemporaries in the comic ſtile; and Sacchini ſeems the moſt promiſing compoſer in the ſerious.

The Honourable Mr. Hamilton, the Britiſh miniſter at this court, whoſe taſte and zeal for the arts, and whoſe patronage of artiſts, are well known throughout Europe, being out of town when I came to Naples, did me the honour, as ſoon as he heard of my arrival, to invite me to his country-houſe, called *Villa Angelica*, at the foot of Mount Veſuvius; and this day, after viſiting Signor Jomelli, I waited upon him for the firſt time, and was received by him and his lady, not only with politeneſs, but even kindneſs. I had the happineſs of continuing there with them two or three days, during which time, among other amuſements, muſic was not wanting, as Mr. Hamilton has two pages of his houſhold, who are excellent performers, one on the violin, and the other on the violoncello.

Saturday 27. This evening, though I had a violent head-ach, yet, in order firſt to brave, and then to ſooth the pain, I determined to try the medicinal power of muſic at Piccini's opera, and found, that though it did not cure, it alleviated the pain, and diverted my attention from it. The houſe was very full, and the actors were in great ſpirits. I went early

early enough, for the firſt time, to hear the overture; it is very pretty and fanciful, conſiſting of only two movements, in which the violins were confined to hard labour. With what pleaſed me before, I was more pleaſed now; it is impoſſible not to be delighted with the originality, and ſurpriſed at the reſources of this author.

Monday 29. Mr. Hamilton being returned to Naples, in order to gratify my muſical curioſity, made a great concert at his houſe, where there was much company, and where I had the ſatisfaction of meeting with the chief muſical performers of this city; among whom were the celebrated player on the violin Signor Barbella, and Orgitano, one of the beſt harpſichord players and writers for that inſtrument at Naples. But Mrs. Hamilton is herſelf a much better performer on that inſtrument than either he or any one I heard there. She has great neatneſs, and more expreſſion and meaning in her playing, than is often found among lady-players; for ladies, it must be owned, though frequently neat in execution, seldom aim at expression. Barbella rather disappointed me; his performance has nothing very surprising in it now: he is not young, indeed; and solo playing is never wanted or regarded here; so that teaching and orchestra playing are his chief employments. He performed, however, most admirably the famous Neapolitan air, which the common people constantly play at Christmas to the Virgin; this he plays with a drone kind of bag-pipe base, in a very humorous though delicate manner. But as a solo player, though his tone is very even and sweet, he is inferior to Nardini, and, indeed, to several others in Italy; but he seems to know music well, and to have a good deal of fancy in his compositions with a tincture of not disagreeable madness.

It was here that I had firſt the honour of being preſented to Lord Fortroſe, from whom I afterwards received many ſingular favours. I was likewiſe introduced to the French Conſul, M. D'Aſtier, who is a real connoiſſeur in muſic; perfectly well acquainted with the different ſtiles of all the great compoſers of Europe, paſt and preſent, and diſcriminates very well in ſpeaking of their ſeveral merits. To him I communicated my plan, and with him I had a very ſatisfactory converſation. In order, I believe, that I might have more time for muſical diſquiſitions with this gentleman, and Signor Barbella, there was a ſupper party ſelected of about ten or twelve, and we ſtaid till near two o'clock in the morning.

Barbella is the beſt natured creature imaginable; his temper, as one of the company obſerved, is as ſoft as the tone of his violin. By ſitting next to him, I acquired much biographical knowledge concerning old Neapolitan muſicians.

Mr. Hamilton had offered to write to all the governors of the ſeveral Conſervatorios, but Signor Barbella very obligingly undertook to get me all the information I could deſire of theſe celebrated muſical ſchools. And Lord Fortroſe, whom he attends every morning, invited me to meet him at his lordſhip's houſe, whenever I pleaſed. So that from Barbella, and a young Engliſhman, Mr. Oliver, who has been four years in the Conſervatorio of St. Onofrio, I obtained a ſatisfactory account of whatever was neceſſary for me to know concerning this part of my buſineſs at Naples. Mr. Hamilton entered ſo far into my views, as to take a liſt of my wants, in order to conſider of the beſt method of getting them ſupplied.

Wedneſday, October 31. This morning I went with young Oliver to his Conſervatorio of St. Onofrio, and viſited all the rooms where the boys practiſe, ſleep, and eat. On the firſt flight of ſtairs was a

trum-

trumpeter, ſcreaming upon his inſtrument till he was ready to burſt; on the ſecond was a French horn, bellowing in the ſame manner. In the common practiſing room there was a *Dutch concert*, conſiſting of ſeven or eight harpſichords, more than as many violins, and ſeveral voices, all performing different things, and in different keys: other boys were writing in the ſame room; but it being holiday time, many were abſent who uſually ſtudy and practiſe in this room. The jumbling them all together in this manner may be convenient for the houſe, and may teach the boys to attend to their own parts with firmneſs, whatever elſe may be going forward at the ſame time; it may likewiſe give them force, by obliging them to play loud in order to hear themſelves; but in the midſt of ſuch jargon, and continued diſſonance, it is wholly impoſſible to give any kind of poliſh or finiſhing to their performance; hence the ſlovenly coarſeneſs ſo remarkable in their public exhibitions; and the total want of taſte, neatneſs, and expreſſion in all theſe young muſicians, till they have acquired them elſewhere.

The beds, which are in the ſame room, ſerve for ſeats to the harpſichords and other inſtruments. Out of thirty or forty boys who were practiſing, I could diſcover but two that were playing the ſame piece: ſome of thoſe who were practiſing on the violin ſeemed to have a great deal of hand. The violoncellos practiſe in another room; and the flutes, hautbois, and other wind inſtruments, in a third, except the trumpets and horns, which are obliged to fag, either on the ſtairs, or on the top of the houſe.

There are in this college ſixteen young *caſtrati*, and theſe lye up ſtairs, by themſelves, in warmer apartments than the other boys, for fear of colds, which might not only render their delicate voices unfit

unfit for exercife at prefent, but hazard the entire lofs of them for ever.

The only vacation in thefe fchools, in the whole year, is in autumn, and that for a few days only: during the winter, the boys rife two hours before it is light, from which time they continue their exercife, an hour and a half at dinner excepted, till eight o'clock at night; and this conftant perfeverance, for a number of years, with genius and good teaching, muft produce great muficians.

After dinner I went to the theatre of St. Carlo, to hear Jomelli's new opera rehearfed. There were only two acts finifhed, but thefe pleafed me much, except the overture, which was fhort, and rather difappointed me, as I expected more would have been made of the firft movement; but as to the fongs and accompanied recitatives, there was merit of fome kind or other in them all, as I hardly remember one that was fo indifferent as not to feize the attention. The ſubject of the opera was Demofoonte; the names of the ſingers I knew not then, except Aprile, the firſt man, and Bianchi, the firſt woman. Aprile has rather a weak and uneven voice, but is conſtantly ſteady, as to intonation. He has a good perſon, a good ſhake, and much taſte and expreſſion. La Bianchi has a ſweet and elegant toned voice, always perfectly in tune, with an admirable portamento; I never heard any one ſing with more eaſe, or in a manner ſo totally free from affectation. The reſt of the vocal performers were all above mediocrity; a tenor with both voice and judgment ſufficient to engage attention; a very fine contr' alto; a young man with a ſoprano voice, whoſe ſinging was full of feeling and expreſſion; and a ſecond woman, whoſe performance was far from deſpicable. Such performers as theſe were neceſſary for the muſic, which is in a difficult ſtile; more full of inſtrumental effects than vocal. Sometimes it may be thought rather laboured,

but

but it is admirable in the *tout enſemble*; maſterly in modulation, and in melody full of new paſſages *. This was the firſt rehearſal, and the inſtruments were rough and unſteady, not being as yet certain of the exact time or expreſſion of the movements; but, as far as I was then able to judge, the compoſition was perfectly ſuited to the talents of the performers, who, though all good, yet not being of the very firſt and moſt exquiſite claſs, were more in want of the aſſiſtance of inſtruments to mark the images, and enforce the paſſion, which the poetry points out.

The public expectation from this production of Jomelli, if a judgment may be formed from the number of perſons who attended this firſt rehearſal, was very great; for the pit was crowded, and many of the boxes were filled with the families of perſons of condition.

* Jomelli is now ſaid to write more for the *learned few*, than for the *feeling many*.

The

The theatre of S. Carlo is a noble and elegant ſtructure: the form is oval, or rather the ſection of an egg, the end next the ſtage being cut. There are ſeven ranges of boxes, ſufficient in ſize to contain ten or twelve perſons in each, who ſit in chairs, in the ſame manner as in a private houſe. In every range there are thirty boxes, except the three loweſt ranges, which, by the king's box being taken out of them, are reduced to twenty-nine. In the pit there are fourteen or fifteen rows of ſeats, which are very roomy and commodious, with leather cuſhions and ſtuffed backs, each ſeparated from the other by a broad reſt for the elbow: in the middle of the pit there are thirty of theſe ſeats in a row.

November 1, being All Saints day, I went, at leaſt two miles, to the church of the Incurabili, where I was told there would be good muſic; but I found it miſerable. From hence I went to ſeveral others, where I only heard bad muſic ill performed.

Friday, Nov. 3. This day I viſited his Neapolitan majeſty's muſeum, at Portici, where I had enquiries to make concerning ancient inſtruments and MSS. which were of real importance to my hiſtory. In the third apartment of this curious repoſitory, where the ancient inſtruments of ſurgery are placed, I met with the following muſical inſtruments; three *Syſtrums*, two with four braſs bars, and one with three; ſeveral *Crotoli* or cymbals; *Tambours de baſque*; a *Syringa*, with ſeven pipes; and a great number of broken bone or ivory *tibiæ*.

But the moſt extraordinary of all theſe inſtruments is a ſpecies of trumpets, found in Pompeia not a year ago; it is a good deal broken, but not ſo much ſo as to render it difficult to conceive the entire form. There are ſtill the remains of ſeven ſmall bone or ivory pipes, which are inſerted in as many of braſs, all of the ſame

ſame length and diameter, which ſurround the great tube, and ſeem to terminate in one mouth-piece. Several of the ſmall brazen pipes are broken, by which the ivory ones are laid bare; but it is natural to ſuppoſe that they were all blown at once, and that the ſmall pipes were uniſons to each other, and octaves to the great one. It uſed to be flung on the ſhoulder by a chain, which chain is preſerved, and the place where it uſed to be faſtened to the trumpet, is ſtill viſible. No ſuch inſtrument as this has been found before, either in ancient painting or ſculpture, which makes me the more minute in ſpeaking of it. This ſingular ſpecies of trumpet was found in the *Corps de Garde*, and ſeems to be the true military "*Clangor Tubarum*."

As no perſon is ſuffered to uſe a pencil in the muſeum, when the company with which I had ſeen it was arrived at the inn where we dined, Mr. Robertſon, an ingenius young artiſt of the party, was ſo obliging

obliging as to make a drawing of it, from memory, in my tablets; which all the company, consisting of seven, agreed was very exact.

In the ninth or tenth room are all the volumes as yet found in Herculaneum, of which only four have been rendered intelligible, these are Greek. One upon the Epicurean philosophy, one upon rhetoric, one upon *morality*, and *one* upon music; each volume appears to be only a black cinder. I saw two pages, opened and framed, of the MS. upon music, written by Philodemus; but it is not a poem on music, as Mr. de la Lande says, nor a satire against it, as others say; but a confutation of the system of Aristoxenus, who, being a practical musician, preferred the judgment of the ear to the Pythagorean numbers, or the arithmetical proportions of mere theorists. Ptolemy did the same afterwards. I conversed with Padre Antonio Pioggi about this MS. it was he who opened and explained it; and he he is now ſuperintending, at a foundery, the caſting of a new ſet of Greek characters exactly, reſembling thoſe in which it was written, and in which it is to be publiſhed.

Every lover of learning laments the ſlow manner in which they proceed in opening theſe volumes. All that have been found hitherto were in Herculaneum. Thoſe of Pompeia are ſuppoſed to have been wholly deſtroyed by fire.

Saturday 3. At night I went to a little neat new play-houſe, juſt opened; there was a comedy in proſe, a Turkiſh ſtory, ill told, and not well acted.

Sunday 4. I went this morning to S. Gennaro, to hear the organ and to ſee the chapel, and the pictures in it, by Dominichini; after which I was conducted to the houſe of Don Carlo Cotumacci, maſter to the Conſervatorio of St. Onofrio, whom I heard play on the harpſichord; and who gave me a great number of anecdotes concerning the muſic of old times. He was ſcholar to the

Cavalier Scarlatti, in the year 1719; and ſhewed me the leſſons he received from that great maſter, in his own hand writing. He alſo gave me a very particular account of Scarlatti and his family. Signor Cotumacci, was Durante's ſucceſſor. He plays, in the old organ ſtile, very full and learnedly, as to modulation; and has compoſed a great deal of church muſic, of which he was ſo obliging as to give me a copy of two or three curious pieces. He has had great experience in teaching; and ſhewed me two books of his own writing, in manuſcript, one upon accompaniment, and one upon counterpoint. I take him to be more than ſeventy years of age.

At night I went to the firſt public repreſentation of Signor Jomelli's opera of *Demofoonte*, in the grand theatre of *San Carlo*, where I was honoured with a place in Mr. Hamilton's box. It is not eaſy to imagine or deſcribe the grandeur and magnificence of this ſpectacle. It being the great feſtival of St. Charles and the

King

King of Spain's name-day, the court was in grand gala, and the houſe was not only doubly illuminated, but amazingly crowded with well-dreſſed company*. In the front of each box there is a mirrour, three or four feet long, by two or three wide, before which are two large wax tapers; theſe, by reflection, being multiplied, and added to the lights of the ſtage and to thoſe within the boxes, make the ſplendor too much for the aching ſight. The King and Queen were preſent. Their Majeſties have a large box in the front of the houſe, which contains in height and breadth the ſpace of four other boxes. The ſtage is of an immenſe ſize, and the ſcenes, dreſſes, and decorations were extremely magnificent; and I think this theatre ſuperior, in theſe particulars, as well as in the muſic, to that of the great French opera at Paris.

* The fourth of November is likewiſe celebrated as the name-day of the Queen of Naples and the Prince of Aſturias.

But M. de la Lande, after allowing that "the opera in Italy is very well as to music and words," concludes with saying "that it is not, in his opinion, quite so in other respects, and for the following reasons;

"1. There is scarce any machinery in the operas of Italy *.

"2. There is not such a multitude of rich and superb dresses as at Paris.

"3. The number and variety of the actors are less †.

"4. The chorusses are fewer and less laboured. And

"5. The union of song and dance is neglected" ‡.

To all which objections, a real lover of music would perhaps say, *so much the better*.

M. de la Lande, however, allows that the hands employed in the orchestra

* The Italians have long given up those puerile representations of flying gods and goddesses, of which the French are still so fond and so vain.

† If the characters are fewer, the dresses must be so, of course.

‡ *Voyage d'un François*, Tom. vi.

are more numerous and various, but complains that the fine voices in an Italian opera are not only too few, but are too much occupied by the musick and its embellishments to attend to declamation and gesture.

With regard to this last charge, it is by no means a just one; for whoever remembers Pertici and Laschi, in the burlettas of London, about twenty years ago, or has seen the Buona Figliuola there lately, when Signora Guadagni, Signor Lovatini, and Signor Morigi were in it; or in the serious operas of past times remembers Monticelli, Elisi, Mingotti, Colomba Mattei, Mansoli, or, above all, in the present operas has seen Signor Guadagni, must allow that many of the Italians, not only recite well, but are *excellent actors*.

Give to a lover of music an opera in a noble theatre, at least twice as large as that of the French capital, in which the poetry and music are good, and the vocal and instrumental parts well performed, and he will deny himself the rest without murmuring; though his ear should be less stunned with chorusses, and his eye less dazzled with machinery, dresses, and dances than at Paris.

But to return to the theatre of S. Carlo, which, as a spectacle, surpasses all that poetry or romance have painted: yet with all this, it must be owned that the magnitude of the building, and noise of the audience are such, that neither the voices or instruments can be heard distinctly. I was told, however, that on account of the King and Queen being present, the people were much less noisy than on common nights. There was not a hand moved by way of applause during the whole representation, though the audience in general seemed pleased with the music: but, to say the truth, it did not afford me the same delight as at the rehearsal; nor did the singers, though they exerted themselves more, appear to equal advantage : not one of the present voices is ſufficiently powerful for ſuch a theatre, when ſo crowded and ſo noiſy. Signora Bianchi, the firſt woman, whoſe ſweet voice and ſimple manner of ſinging gave me and others ſo much pleaſure at the rehearſal, did not ſatisfy the Neapolitans, who have been accuſtomed to the force and brilliancy of a Gabrieli, a Taiber, and a de Amici. There is too much ſimplicity in her manner for the depraved appetites of theſe *enfans gatés*, who are never pleaſed but when aſtoniſhed. As to the muſic, much of the *claire obſcure* was loſt, and nothing could be heard diſtinctly but thoſe noiſy and furious parts which were meant merely to give *relief* to the reſt ; the mezzotints and back-ground were generally loſt, and indeed little was left but the bold and coarſe ſtrokes of the compoſer's pencil.

During the performance, Caffarelli came into the pit, and Signor Giraldi, who was in Mr. Hamilton's box, proposed to make us acquainted; and at the end of the performance, he conducted me to him; he looks well, and has a very lively and animated countenance; he does not seem to be above fifty years of age, though he is said to be sixty-three. He was very polite, and entered into conversation with great ease and chearfulness; he enquired after the Duchess of Manchester, and Lady Fanny Shirley, who had honoured him with their protection when he was in England, which, he said, was in the end of Mr. Heydegger's reign. He introduced me to Signor Gennaro Manno, a celebrated Neapolitan composer, who sat behind him. Signor Giraldi had been with him before, to fix a time for bringing me to his house; it was now settled that we should meet at Lord Fortrose's; indeed it was to his Lordship that I was indebted for this, and for many other opportunities of information at Naples.

The houſe was emptying very faſt, and I was obliged to take my leave of this ſire of ſong, who is the oldeſt ſinger in Europe that continues the public exerciſe of his profeſſion ; for he frequently ſings in convents and in churches yet, though he has for ſome time quitted the ſtage.

In the opera to-night there were three entertaining dances, but all in the lively way ; the Italians are not pleaſed with any other. Indeed, as I have before obſerved, all their dances are more pantomime entertainments than any thing elſe, in which the ſcenes are uſually pretty, and the ſtories well told. The ſubject of the firſt dance was *l'iſola diſabitata* ; of the ſecond, the humours of Vauxhall Gardens in England, in which were introduced quakers, ſailors, women of the town, Savoyard ſhew-boxes, &c. and in the third dance, at the end of the piece, the people of Thrace figured at the nuptials of Creuſa and Cherinto, characters of the opera. The ſix principal

dancers

dancers among the men are *gli Signori Onocuto Vigano, Giuſeppe Traſieri, Franceſco Raſetti*; and among the women, *le Signore Colomba Beccari, Anna Torſelli,* and *Caterina Ricci*; the firſt man has great force and neatneſs, and ſeems to equal Slingſby in his *à plomb*, or neatneſs of keeping time; and the Beccari's *many twinkling feet* are not inferior in agility to thoſe of Radicate.

Monday 5. This morning I went to the Conſervatorio of St. Onofrio, to ſee the boys take their leſſons, and to hear ſome of the beſt of them play; they were all hard at work, and a noble clangor they made, not to be equalled by

A hundred mouths, a hundred tongues,
A hundred pair of iron lungs,
Ten ſpeaking trumpets, &c.

However, the ears of both maſter and ſcholar are reſpected when leſſons in ſinging are given, for that work is done in a quiet room; but in the common practiſing rooms the noiſe and diſſonance are beyond all conception. However, I heard in a private room two of the boys accompany each other; the one played a ſolo of Giardini's on the violin, and the other one of his own on the baſe; the firſt was but indifferently executed, but the ſecond was a pretty compoſition, and very well performed. I find all over Italy that Giardini's ſolos, and Bach's and Abel's overtures, are in great repute, and very juſty ſo, as I heard nothing equal to them of the kind, on the continent.

From hence I went to ſee a great feſtival at the convent of *la Donna Regina*, it was *una belliſſima Funzione*, as the Italians call it, on account of two Turkiſh ſlaves, who being converted to the Chriſtian religion, were this day publicly baptiſed: ſeveral biſhops aſſiſted at the ceremony, and the church was crowded with the beſt company of Naples. The muſic was compoſed by Giuſeppe da Majo, a Neapolitan

litan compoſer, brought up in the Conſervatorio of the *Pietà*, and was excellent, though coarſely performed.

Having the honour, to-day, of dining at our miniſter's, I was very much entertained in the afternoon by the performance of a fat friar, of the order of St. Dominic, who came there to ſing *bùffo* ſongs; he accompanied himſelf on the harpſichord in a great number of humorous ſcenes from the burletta operas of Piccini and Paeſiello, which he ſung with a comic force, little inferior to that of Caſaccia, and with a much better voice.

Signor Naſci, who leads the band at the comic opera in the theatre *de Fiorentini*, played on the violin in the Dominican's performance, and afterward in ſome of his own trios, which are extremely pretty, with a very uncommon degree of grace and facility.

After this Mr. Hamilton was ſo obliging as to ſhew me his charming picture, painted

painted by Correggio; the ſubject is a naked Venus who has taken Cupid's bow from him, which he is ſtruggling for, while a ſatyr is running away with his quiver. It is a wonderful performance, and reckoned equal, for the number of figures, to the St. Jerome, at Parma.

The curioſities both of art and nature in Mr. Hamilton's poſſeſſion, are numberleſs and ineſtimable. The examination of his immenſe collection of Etruſcan vaſes, and other rarities of the higheſt antiquity, was of the utmoſt importance to the ſubject of my enquiries. But by theſe precious remains of art I was not more enlightened, concerning the muſic and inſtruments of the ancients, than by his converſation and counſel.

When we returned to the apartments which we had quitted, in order to viſit the library, we found a Neapolitan Prince and Princeſs, two or three ambaſſadors, Lord Fortroſe, the French conſul, a number of Engliſh gentlemen, and much other com-

company; in the evening there was more music, and at supper a select party, which did not separate till two o'clock in the morning, when I took leave of Mr. Hamilton and his lady with infinite regret, as the countenance and assistance with which I was honoured by them, during my residence at Naples, were not only of the utmost utility to me and my plan, but such as gratitude will never suffer me to forget.

Tuesday 6. This day I had the honour of dining with Lord Fortrose; the company was very numerous, and chiefly musical. Barbella and Orgitano were invited; there was likewise the French consul, M. D'Astier. After dinner, a complete band was assembled in the gallery, and we had music till past eleven o'clock. Barbella pleased me much more to-night than he had done before; he is very certain of his tone, and has a great deal of taste and expression; if he had a little more brilliancy and fullness of tone, and a

greater

greater variety of ſtile, his playing would be unexceptionable, and perhaps ſuperior to that of moſt players in Europe: as it is, there ſeems to be a drowſineſs in his tone, and a want of animation in his manner.

Orgitano played the harpſichord, and Signor Conſorte, a *muſico*, was there to ſing; there was likewiſe a pretty good ſolo hautbois. The whole company had given Caffarelli over, when, behold! he arrived in great good humour; and, contrary to all expectation, was, with little entreaty, prevailed upon to ſing. Many notes in his voice are now thin, but there are ſtill traits in his performance ſufficient to convince thoſe who hear him, of his having been an amazing fine ſinger; he accompanied himſelf, and ſung without any other inſtrument than the harpſichord; expreſſion and grace, with great neatneſs in all he attempts, are his characteriſtics. Though Caffarelli and Barbella

bella are rather ancient and in ruin, yet what remains of them is but the more precious. Caffarelli propofed our fpending a whole day together, in order to difcufs mufical matters, and faid it would even be too little for all that we had to fay; but when I had acquainted him of the neceffity I was under of fetting out for Rome the next night, immediately after the opera, he offered to meet me again at Lord Fortrofe's the next morning.

After fupper, Barbella played extremely well feveral Calabrefe, Leccefe, and Neapolitan airs, and among the reft, a humourous piece compofed by himfelf, which he calls *ninna nonna*; it is a nurfery tune, or *lullaby*, excellent in its way, and was well expreffed.

Wednefday 7. I vifited by appointment, Padre della Torre, to whom I had letters; he is librarian to the king, and keeper of his majefty's cabinet of rarities at the foot of Capo di Monte. I never

never ſaw one of a more chearfully obliging character. He cannot be leſs than 70 years of age, and yet he is as lively, and even ſportive, as a young man of 20. He and his aſſiſtant had been hunting with great diligence in the king's library, which formerly belonged to the Farneſe family, and was brought hither from Parma, for materials relative to muſic. He ſhewed me, among ſeveral books and MSS which I already knew, ſome curious inedited tracts which are no where elſe to be found *.

After this, he ſhewed me his microſcopes and teleſcopes, which are famous all over Italy; this father being ſaid to have made great improvements in both, but eſpecially in microſcopes, by means of a very ſmall drop or globule of pure chryſtal glaſs, the ſmaller the better.

* There is a diſſertation upon ſound in his own works collected and publiſhed in 9 vols. 8vo. under this title—*Elementa Phyſicæ, auctore P. D. Johanne Maria de Terre. Napoli,* 1769.

He

He melts the glaſs himſelf in a veſſel of Tripoli earth, and renders it ſpherical in a clear flame. It magnifies the diameter of an object, if the globule be of the ſmalleſt claſs, 2560 times; the common microſcopes only magnify about 350 times †. After ſhewing me the whole proceſs, he was ſo obliging as to furniſh me with ſeveral of theſe glaſs globules for my own uſe.

From hence I went to the houſe of Lord Fortroſe, to meet Caffarelli; and

† The diſcovery is not new; Leeuwenhoek is ſaid to have uſed little ſpheres of glaſs in his microſcopes; Mr. Baker indeed treats them with contempt: and ſays, "Experience has taught, that they admit ſo little light, can ſhew ſuch an exceedingly ſmall part of any object, are ſo difficult to make uſe of, and ſtrain the eyes ſo much, that their power of magnifying for want of due diſtinctneſs, is rather apt to produce error than diſcover truth." *Microſcope made eaſy.* But however true this might have been at the time Mr. Baker wrote, *Padre della Torre* ſeems at preſent to have got the better of every objection to theſe glaſs globules by the dexterity with which he forms and uſes them.

now I have mentioned his name for the laſt time, it affords me an opportunity of acquainting my reader, that this celebrated ſinger has bought a dukedom for his nephew, after his own deceaſe, the title is *Duca di Santi Dorato*. He is very rich, yet often ſings for hire at convents and at churches. He has built himſelf a magnificent houſe, and over the door is this inſcription:

AMPHION THEBAS, EGO DOMVM*.

To-day I was favoured at dinner with the company of Signor Fabio, the firſt violin of the opera of S. Carlo; he was ſo obliging and ſo humble as to bring with him his violin. It is very common in the great cities of Italy to ſee performers of the firſt eminence carry their own inſtruments through the ſtreets. This ſeems a trivial circumſtance to mention, yet it ſtrongly marks the difference of manners and characters in two

* Amphion built Thebes, I only a houſe.

countries not very remote from each other, In Italy, the leader of the firſt opera in the world carries the inſtrument of his fame and fortune about him, with as much pride as a ſoldier does his ſword or muſquet; while, in England, the indignities he would receive from the populace would ſoon impreſs his mind with ſhame for himſelf and fear for his inſtrument.

I obtained from Signor Fabio an exact account of the number of hands employed in the great opera orcheſtra: there are 18 firſt, and 18 ſecond violins, 5 double baſes, and but 2 violoncellos; which I think has a bad effect, the double baſe being played ſo coarſely throughout Italy, that it produces a ſound no more muſical than the ſtroke of a hammer. This performer, who is a fat, good-natured man, by being long accuſtomed to lead ſo great a number of hands, has acquired a ſtile of playing, which is ſomewhat rough and inelegant, and conſequently more fit for an orcheſtra than a chamber. He ſung, however, ſeveral buffo ſongs very well, and accompanied himſelf on the violin in ſo maſterly a manner, as to produce moſt of the effects of a numerous band. After dinner, he had a ſecond to accompany him in one of Giardini's ſolos, and in ſeveral other things.

I ſpent this whole evening with Barbella, who now delivered to me all the materials which he had been able to collect, relative to a hiſtory of the Neapolitan conſervatorios, as well as anecdotes of the old compoſers and performers of that ſchool: beſides theſe, I wrote down all the verbal information I could extract from his memory, concerning muſical perſons and things. During my viſit, I heard one of his beſt ſcholars play a ſolo of Giardini's compoſition very well; he was the moſt brilliant performer on the violin that I met with at Naples.

And now, having given the reader an account of the muſical entertainment I received at Naples, I hope I ſhall be indulged with the liberty of making a few reflexions before I quit this city; which has ſo long been regarded as the centre of harmony, and the fountain from whence genius, taſte, and learning, have flowed to every other part of Europe; that even theſe who have an opportunity of judging for themſelves, take upon truſt the truth of the fact, and give the Neapolitans credit for more than they deſerve at preſent, however they may have been entitled to this celebrity in times paſt.

M. de la Lande's account of muſic at Naples, is ſo far from exact, that it would incline his reader to ſuppoſe one of two things, either that he did not attend to it, or that he had not a very diſtinguiſhing ear.

" Muſic, ſays this author, is in a par-" ticular manner the triumph of the" Neapolitans; it ſeems as if the tym-" panum in this country was more bra-

" ced, more harmonical, and more ſono-" rous, than in the reſt of Europe; the " whole nation is vocal, every geſture " and inflexion of voice of the inhabi-" tants, and even their proſody of ſyl-" lables in converſation, breathe har-" mony and muſic. Hence Naples is " the principal ſource of Italian muſic, " of great compoſers, and of excellent " operas *."

I am ready to grant that the Neapolitans have a natural diſpoſition to muſic; but can by no means allow that they have voices more flexible, and a language more harmonious than the inhabitants of the other parts of Italy, as the direct contrary ſeems true. The ſinging in the

* *Voyage du'n François*, Tom. 6. The inaccuracy with which M. de la L. ſpeaks about muſic and muſicians, runs through his work. He places Corelli and Galuppi among the Neapolitan Compoſers; whereas it is well known that Corelli was of the Roman ſchool, and he himſelf ſays in another place (Tom. 5.) that Galuppi was of the Venetian.

ſtreets is far leſs pleaſing, though more original than elſewhere ; and the Neapolitan language is generally ſaid to be the moſt barbarous jargon among all the different dialects of Italy *.

But though the riſing generation of Neapolitan muſicians cannot be ſaid to poſſeſs either taſte, delicacy, or expreſſion, yet their compoſitions, it muſt be allowed, are excellent with reſpect to counter-point and invention ; and in their manner of executing them, there is an energy and fire, not to be met with perhaps in the whole univerſe : it is ſo ardent as to border upon fury ; and from this impetuoſity of genius, it is common for a Neapolitan compoſer, in a movement which begins in a mild and ſober manner, to ſet the orcheſtra in

* A ſufficient proof of the Neapolitan language being only a *patois* or provincial dialect, is, that it remains merely oral, the natives themſelves, who are well educated, never daring to write in it.

flames before it is finiſhed. Dr. Johnſon ſays, that Shakeſpeare, in tragedy, is always ſtruggling after ſome occaſion to be comic; and the Neapolitans, like high bred horſes, are impatient of the rein, and eagerly accelerate their motion to the utmoſt of their ſpeed. The pathetic and the graceful are ſeldom attempted in the conſervatorios; and thoſe refined and ſtudied graces, which not only change, but improve paſſages, and which ſo few are able to find, are leſs ſought after by the generality of performers at Naples, than in any other part of Italy.

R O M E.

Sunday, Nov. 11. Having a little recovered the fatigue of my journey from Naples, I renewed my operations at Rome.

This morning I went to the convent of St. Urſula, to ſee a nun take the veil.

The company was very numerous, and composed chiefly of the first people of Rome, who were all in full dress. I was placed close to the altar, where I could see the whole ceremony, and hear every word that was uttered. The service was begun by saying mass, then cardinal de Rossi entered in great state; while the organ was playing, and the mass was singing: the music both vocal and instrumental, was performed by the nuns and ladies of the convent, who were placed in the organ gallery. The composition was pretty, but ill executed; the organ was a bad one, and too powerful for the band: most of the best hands, as I was informed, were occupied in the convent with the internal ceremony, the external was all performed in the chapel.

When the cardinal was robed, the noviciate was led into the chapel by a lady of the first rank in Rome, and brought to the altar in exceeding high dress. Her hair was of a beautiful light brown, and curled *en tête de mouton* all over her head. Her gown was of the richest embroidered, and, I believe, embossed blue and silver, I ever saw. She had on a large stage hoop, and a great quantity of diamonds; the train of her robe dragged full two yards on the ground; she seemed rather a pretty sort of young person than a beauty. When she first appeared, she looked very pale, and more dead than alive; she made a most profound reverence to the cardinal, who was seated on the steps of the altar in his mitre and all his rich vestments, ready to receive her. She threw herself upon her knees at the foot of the altar, and remained in that posture some time, while other parts of the ceremony were adjusting; then she walked up to the cardinal, who said, *Figlia mia, che domandate?* My child, what is your request? She said, that she begged to be admitted into that convent as a sister of the order of St. Ursula: Have you well, said the cardinal, considered of what you

ask?

aſk? She anſwered, cheafully, that ſhe had; and was well informed of all ſhe was about to do. Then ſhe kneeled down again, and kiſſed the cardinal's hands, and received from him a little crucifix, which ſhe alſo kiſſed; after which ſhe retired again to the foot of the altar, where ſhe threw herſelf on her knees, while the cardinal ſaid maſs, which was ſung at the ſame time in the organ loft. After this, there was a ſermon in the Italian language, and that being over, the cardinal led the nun-elect into the convent, where ſhe was diveſted of all her gorgeous attire and worldly vanities, and had her hair cut off. She then came to the gate in her religious dreſs, to receive the white veil, with which ſhe was inveſted by the lady abbeſs, the cardinal and the other aſſiſtants ſtanding by.

After this there was more pretty muſic badly performed. The organ, by executing all the ſymphonies and accompaniments,

ments, overpowered the violins, and had a bad effect, though neatly played.

When her veil was on, the new ſiſter came to the convent door, to receive the congratulations of her friends and of the company; but firſt, with a lighted taper in her hand, ſhe went round the convent to ſalute all the nuns, who had likewiſe tapers in their hands. When ſhe was at the door, with the veil and crown on, but her face uncovered, I, among the reſt, went cloſe to her, and found ſhe was much prettier than I had before imagined. She had a ſweet mouth, and the fineſt teeth in the world, with lively ſparkling eyes, and a genteel ſhaped viſage; ſhe would, any where elſe, have been ſtiled a very pretty woman; but here, ſo circumſtanced, a beauty. At the altar ſhe changed countenance ſeveral times, firſt pale, then red, and ſeemed to pant, and to be in danger of either burſting into tears, or fainting; but ſhe recovered before the ceremony was ended, and at the

convent

convent door aſſumed an air of great chearfulneſs; talked to ſeveral of her friends and acquaintance, and ſeemed to give up the world very heroically.—And thus ended this human ſacrifice!

In the afternoon I went to the Chieſa Nuova, to hear an oratorio in that church, where the ſacred drama took its riſe. There are two galleries; in one there is an organ, and in the other a harpſichord; in the former the ſervice was begun by the matins in four parts, *alla Paleſtrina*; then the *Salve Regina* was ſung *a voce ſola*, after which there were prayers; and then a little boy, not above ſix years old, mounted the pulpit, and delivered a diſcourſe, by way of ſermon, which he had got by heart, and which was rendered truly ridiculous by the vehicle through which it paſſed. The oratorio of Abigail, ſet to muſic by Signor Caſali, was then performed. This drama conſiſted of four characters, and was divided into two parts. The two firſt move-

movements of the overture pleaſed me very much, the laſt not at all. It was, as uſual, a minuet degenerated into a jigg of the moſt common caſt. This rapidity in the minuets of all modern overtures renders them ungraceful at an opera, but in a church they are indecent. The reſt of the muſic was pretty common place, for though it could boaſt of no new melody or modulation, it had nothing vulgar in it.

Signor Criſtofero ſung the principal part very well, in Guarducci's ſmooth and poliſhed manner. He made two or three excellent cloſes, though they were rather too long; this fault is general throughout Rome and Naples, where ſuch a long-winded licentiouſneſs prevails in the cadences of every ſinger, as is always tireſome, and often diſguſting; even thoſe of great performers need compreſſion, and thoſe made by performers of an inferior claſs not only want curtailing, but correction. A few ſelect notes

with

with a great deal of meaning and expreſſion given to them, is the only expedient that can render a cadence deſirable, as it ſhould conſiſt of ſomething *ſuperior* to what has been heard in the air, or it becomes impertinent. This abuſe in making cloſes is not of very ancient ſtanding, for in a ſerious opera of old Scarlatti, compoſed in 1717, there is not a ſingle place for a cadence *ad libitum* to be found.

Between the two parts of this oratorio, there was a ſermon by a Jeſuit, delivered from the ſame pulpit from whence the child had deſcended. I waited to hear the laſt chorus, which, though it was ſung by book, was as light and as unmeaning as an opera chorus, which muſt be got by heart. With reſpect to a true oratorio chorus accompanied with inſtruments in the manner of Handel's, I heard but few all the time I was in Italy. When this performance was over, I went, as ufual, to the Duke of Dorfet's concert.

Monday 12. I vifited the Pope's, or Siftine chapel, and being a day in which there was no fervice, I had permiffion to go into every part of it, which I was curious to do on many accounts. Firft, as it was the place in which the famous *Miferere* of Allegri is performed; fecondly, as it was here that church-mufic firft had its rife, and was brought to its higheft perfection; and thirdly, where, at the altar piece, is fo wonderfully painted the laft judgment: it is the greateft work of Michael Angelo, and perhaps of man. Nothing can be conceived more aftonifhing and dreadful than the ideas and figures which his dark imagination has produced: neither the *Inferno* of Dante, nor the hell of Milton, can furnifh any thing more terrible. But this amazing work is greatly difcoloured, and the ceiling, by the fame painter, is in many places

places broken down two or three feet in breadth. The ſides are painted by Pietro Perugino, and are the beſt works I have ſeen of this famous maſter of the divine Raphael.

I went up into the orcheſtra with reſpectful curioſity, to ſee the place ſacred to the works of Paleſtrina. It ſeems hardly large enough to contain thirty performers, the ordinary number of ſingers in the Pope's ſervice; and yet, on great feſtivals, ſupernumeraries are added to theſe. There was nothing in the orcheſtra now but a large wooden deſk, for the ſcore book of the maeſtro di Capella, and marble ſeats at the back and ſides: it is placed on the right hand in approaching the altar, facing the Pope's throne, which is near the altar on the other ſide. There are ſeats or ſtalls for the cardinals at the ſides of the chapel and a ſmall place for ambaſſadors to ſtand in, juſt within the rails oppoſite to the altar; but no other ſtrangers are ever admitted; nor are any perſons, except the performers, ſuffered

ſuffered to enter the orcheſtra during the ſervice. The grate, or baluſtrade, which is in diamond ſquares, gilt, ſeems to take off one third of the whole room, which is very lofty and magnificent, but now very duſty and much out of repair; the floor is in beautiful Moſaic of marble.

From hence I went to the Pauline chapel, which is uſed only once a year, at which time it is illuminated with many thouſand lamps.

In the afternoon I had the pleaſure of ſeeing my very good friend Signor Santarelli, who had not only buſied himſelf in ſeeking curious things for me during my abſence at Naples, but had employed ſeveral perſons in tranſcribing them; the Abate Elie had done the ſame at the Vatican; and the Cavalier Piraneſi, my Engliſh friends, and ſeveral eminent antiquaries and artiſts had been active in ſearching ancient inſtruments, among the *baſſi rilievi* and beſt ſculptures of antiquity, and copying them ready for me at my

return

return to Rome. Signor Santarelli was ſo obliging as to accompany me to the Cavalier Battoni's, where his ſcholar, the Signorina Battoni, ſung with noble ſimplicity, and a truly pathetic expreſſion, ſeveral ſongs of Haſſe, Galuppi, Traetta, and Piccini.

From hence I went to a great concert, at the houſe of M. Schovelhoffe, the Moſcovite general; and there I almoſt fancied myſelf in London; for, except three or four, the whole company, conſiſting of near thirty noblemen, gentlemen, and ladies, was Engliſh. The little Mignatrici, Bichelli, was there to ſing, and another girl; the former ſung very well, and the other *will* ſing, ſome time hence: there was nothing extraordinary in the inſtruments.

Tueſday 13. I had but juſt time to ſtep into the beautiful little church of St. Andrea della Noviciata, built by Bernini, at which there was muſic compoſed by Oriſicchio, and led by Nicolai;

 but,

but, though my ſtay was very ſhort, I heard a *ſinfonia* or overture, and a chorus a *due cori*, which were excellent*.

Friday 16. In a viſit I made Signor Santarelli this morning, I found with him three or four of his brethren of the pope's chapel; among the reſt, Signor Paſquale Piſari, who had with him the original ſcore of a maſs in 16 real parts, which was full of canons, fugues, and imitations: I never ſaw a more learned or ingenious compoſition of the kind. Paleſtrina never wrote in more than eight real parts, and few have ſucceeded in ſo many as thoſe; but to double the number is infinitely more than doubling the difficulties. After three parts, the addition of another becomes more and more difficult; all that can be done on theſe occaſions, is to adhere to a ſimple melody

* Signor Orificchio ranks ſo high among the preſent Roman compoſers for the church, that upon any feſtival wherever he is Maeſtro di Capella, and has compoſed a maſs, there is ſure to be a very great crowd.

and modulation, and to keep the parts as much as poſſible in contrary, or at leaſt, diſſimilar motion. In the compoſition of Signor Piſari, every ſpecies of contrivance is ſucceſsfully uſed. Sometimes the parts anſwer or imitate each other, by two and two; ſometimes the ſubjects are inverted in ſome of the parts, while their original order is preſerved in others. A century or two ago, the author of ſuch a compoſition would have had a ſtatue erected to his honour; but now, it would be equally difficult to find 16 people who would hear it with patience, as that number of good ſingers, in any one place, to perform it. Beſides vocal parts in this maſs, there is a part for the organ, often on a regular ſubject, different from the reſt: the groundwork, upon which all is built, is *canto fermo*; and, in ſome of the movements, this canto fermo is made a ſubject of imitation, and runs through all the parts. Upon the whole, it muſt be al-

allowed, that this work, which consists of many different movements, and is of a very considerable length, though it may be thought by some to require more patience than genius to accomplish, seems sufficient to have employed a long life in composing, and to entitle the author to great praise and admiration.

During this visit, which was my last to Signor Santarelli, he and his brethren of the pope's chapel, were so obliging as to execute several beautiful compositions of Palestrina, Benevoli, and Allegri, in order to give me a true idea of the delicate and expressive manner in which they are sung in the chapel of his holiness.

In the afternoon I went to Signor Crispi's *accademia*; I arrived late, while some new *Quartettos* of his composition were performing; but he was so obliging as to desire the band to begin again, and to go through with the whole six. I think these pieces have great merit, and are superior to any of his other productions.

Sunday 18. I went this morning with Mr. Wyſeman to the church of S. John Lateran *; it is the moſt antient church in Chriſtendom. I here heard high maſs performed in the Colonna chapel, by two choirs, and ſaw it played by Signor Coliſta, the celebrated organiſt of that church, on a little moveable organ. The muſic was by Signor Caſali, Maeſtro di Capella, who was there to beat time. I was introduced both to him and to Signor Coliſta, after the ſervice; and the latter upon being entreated to let me hear the great organ, very obligingly conſented,

* Mr. Wyſeman is a worthy Engliſh muſic-maſter, who is well known and eſteemed by all the Engliſh at Rome, where he has ſo long been an inhabitant, that he has almoſt forgot his native tongue. He now lives in the *Palazzo Rafaele*, without the gates of Rome; where, during the firſt winter months, he has a concert every week till the operas begin. It was here that the great Raphael lived, where there are ſtill ſome of his paintings in freſco; and where the late Duke of York, the Prince of Brunſwick, and ſeveral other great perſonages, gave concerts to the firſt people of Rome.

upon condition that *Monſignore il Prefetto* of the church was applied to; which is a neceſſary ceremony in conſequence of ſome injury formerly done to the inſtrument, by the malice or ignorance of a ſtranger who had played upon it. This application was readily undertaken, and the permiſſion obtained, by Signor Caſali.

I was conducted into the great organ-loft by Signor Coliſta, who did me the favour to open the caſe, and to ſhew me all the internal conſtruction of this famous inſtrument. It is a thirty-two feet organ, and the largeſt in Rome. It was firſt built in 1549, and has undergone two repairs ſince; the one in 1600, by Luca Blaſi Perugino; and a ſecond, a few years ſince, under the direction of the preſent organiſt. It has thirty-ſix ſtops, two ſets of keys, long eighths, an octave below double F. and goes up to E. in altiſſimo. It has likewiſe pedals; in the uſe of which Signor Coliſta is very dextrous.

trous. His manner of playing this inftrument feems to be the true organ ftile, though his tafte is rather ancient; indeed the organ ftile feems to be better preferved throughout Italy than it is with us; as the harpfichord is not fufficiently cultivated to encroach upon that inftrument. Signor Colifta played feveral fugues, in which the fubjects were frequently introduced on the pedals, in a very mafterly manner. But it feems as if every virtue in mufic was to border upon fome vice; for this ftile of playing precludes all grace, tafte, and melody; while the light, airy harpfichord kind of playing, deftroys the *foftenuto* and richnefs of harmony and contrivance of which this divine inftrument is fo peculiarly capable.

It is very extraordinary that the *fwell*, which has been introduced into the Englifh organ more than fifty years, and which is fo capable of expreffion and of pleafing effects, that it may well be faid to be the greateſt and moſt important improvement that ever was made on any keyed inſtrument, ſhould be ſtill utterly unknown in Italy*. The *touch* too of the organ, which our builders have ſo much improved, ſtill remains in its heavy, noiſy ſtate; and now I am on this ſubject, I muſt obſerve, that moſt of the organs I have met with on the Continent, ſeem to be inferior to ours built by father Smith, Byfield, or Snetzler, in every thing but ſize. As the churches there are often immenſe, ſo are the organs; the tone is indeed ſomewhat ſoftened and refined by ſpace and diſtance; but when heard near, it is intolerably coarſe and noiſy; and though the number of ſtops in theſe

* It is the ſame with the *Beat* upon the uniſon, octave, or any conſonant ſound to a note on the violin, which ſo well ſupplies the place of the old cloſe-ſhake: for this beautiful effect, if not wholly unknown, is at leaſt neglected by all the violin performers I heard on the continent, though ſo commonly and ſucceſsfully practiſed in England by thoſe of the Giardini ſchool.

large

large inſtruments is very great, they afford but little variety, being, for the moſt part, duplicates in uniſons and octaves to each other, ſuch as the great and ſmall 12ths, flutes, and 15ths: hence in our organs not only the touch and tone, but the imitative ſtops are greatly ſuperior to thoſe of any other organs I have met with.

Immediately after dinner I went to St. Peter's, where there was a great *Funzione* for the feaſt of it's foundation. The veſpers were ſaid by Cardinal York, aſſiſted by ſeveral biſhops: there were Mazzanti and Criſtofero to ſing, beſides ſeveral other ſupernumeraries, and the whole choir. The fat Giovannini, famous for playing the violoncello, as well as for being one of the *maeſtri di capella* of St. Peter's, beat time. The ſolo parts were finely ſung by the two ſingers juſt mentioned, and the choruſſes by two choirs, and two organs, were admirably performed. Part of the muſic was by Paleſtrina, part by Benevoli, and the reſt modern, but in a grave and majeſtic

majeſtic ſtile. I never heard church muſic, except that of the Pope's chapel, ſo well performed. There were no other inſtruments than the two organs, four violoncellos, and two double baſes. Some fugues and imitations in dialogue between the two choirs were performed, which had a very fine effect. The ſervice was in the large canonical, or winter chapel on the left, in which is the largeſt organ of St. Peter's church *.

Cardinal York ſaid maſs likewiſe in the morning, when there was a great congregation.

At night I went to the oratorio of Jonathan, at the Chieſa Nuova; but not being either well ſet or well ſung, I quitted that performance at the end of the firſt part, in order to hear another at the church of St. Gerolamo della Carità,

* There are no other organs, nor indeed choirs at St. Peter's than thoſe in the ſide chapels; ſo that the diſtance between the weſt door and the great altar, is wholly a free and unbroken ſpace.

which had only three characters in it: this oratorio was called the Judgment of Solomon: the tenor finger in it was admirable; he had great tafte, and a very uncommon facility of execution: a eunuch likewife, who performed the part of one of the mothers, had a fweet toned voice, and fung in a very pleafing manner. The fubject feems to be extremely well adapted for mufical expreffion: the fternnefs of the judge; the indifference of the falfe mother; and the tendernefs of the true, are feverally fufceptible of different mufical colouring and expreffion. The mufic, which had merit, was by a young compofer who had begged employment in order to have an opportunity of difplaying his talents: his name is Giufeppe Maria Magherini.

Tuefday 20. I went this morning to vifit the famous Podini gallery, in the Verufpi palace. All the accounts of Rome are full of the praifes of this mufic gallery; or, as it is called, gallery of inftruments;

ments; but nothing ſhews the neceſſity of ſeeing for one's ſelf, more than theſe accounts. The inſtruments in queſtion cannot have been fit for uſe theſe many years; but, when a thing has once got into a book as curious, it is copied into others without examination, and without end. There is a very fine harpſichord, to look at, but not a key that will ſpeak: it formerly had a communication with an organ in the ſame room, and with two ſpinets and a virginal; under the frame is a violin, tenor, and baſe, which, by a movement of the foot, uſed to be played upon by the harpſichord keys. The organ appears in the front of the room, but not on the ſide, where there ſeems to be pipes and machines encloſed; but there was no one to open or explain it, the old *Ciceroni* being juſt dead.

Wedneſday 21. This morning I went to the Kirkeana muſeum, founded about the middle of the laſt century by Father Kircher, author of the *Muſurgia*, and of ſeveral

ſeveral other curious and learned works. Mr. Morriſon, who had obtained permiſſion for me to ſee it, was ſo obliging as to accompany me thither. The muſeo was ſhewn us by a young Iriſh jeſuit, Father Plunket, I think, who is likewiſe a young antiquary; but Mr. Morriſon, who is undoubtedly one of the firſt and moſt ſagacious antiquaries in Rome, ſet him right in many particulars. Ancient paintings, urns, vaſes, jewels, intaglios, cameos, and other antiquities, are here in ſuch abundance, that I could have fancied myſelf at Portici; but the curioſities I chiefly went to ſee, were Father Kircher's muſical inſtruments and machines, deſcribed in his *Muſurgia:* they are now almoſt all out of order, but their conſtruction is really curious, and manifeſts the ingenuity as well as zeal of this learned father in his muſical enquiries and experiments.

In viſiting Rome a ſecond time, I took a view of the theatres, of which there are ſeven or eight: the principal are the *Argentina*, the *Aliberti*, the *Pordinone*, and the *Capranica:* the two firſt are very large, and appropriated to ſerious operas. The *Pordenone* theatre is uſed as a playhouſe for tragedies and comedies; and the *Capranica* for burlettas, or comic operas.

There are no public ſpectacles allowed in Rome, except during carnival time, which laſts from the ſeventh of January to Aſh-Wedneſday; nor are any women ever ſuffered to appear upon the ſtage, the female characters being repreſented by eunuchs, and frequently ſo well, from their delicacy of voice and figure, as to deceive perſons unacquainted with this prohibition.

Rome is the poſt of honour for compoſers, the Romans being the moſt faſtidious judges of muſic in Italy. There is likewiſe in this city more cabal than elſewhere, and party runs higher. It is generally ſuppoſed, that a compoſer or performer who

who is ſucceſsful at Rome, has nothing to fear from the ſeverity of critics in other places. At the opening of an opera, the clamour or acclamation of the company frequently continues for a conſiderable time before they will hear a note. A favourite author is received with ſhouts of *Bravo! Signor Maeſtro. Viva! Signor Maeſtro.* And when a compoſer is condemned by the audience, it is with diſcrimination in favour of the ſinger, by crying out, after they have done hiſſing, *Bravo! pure, il Guarducci *!* and on the contrary, if the performer diſpleaſes in executing the muſic of a favourite compoſer, after they have expreſſed their diſapprobation of him, by hiſſing, they cry out *Viva! pure, il Signor Maeſtro.*

It was with much regret that I quitted this venerable city, which is no leſs delightful to ſtrangers for the innumerable rarities it offers to their view, than for

* Bravo! however, Guarducci.

the eaſy and ſocial manner in which they live with the natives, as well as with each other.

I have now given an account of the ſtate of muſic in the principal cities of Italy; there are, however, many places which I either was unable to viſit, or in which my ſtay was too ſhort to obtain much information; however, the following particulars ſeem worthy of being mentioned: at Loretto there is a conſiderable muſic ſchool: at Siena there are curious miſſals: at Piſa, muſic is in a flouriſhing ſtate, as I was informed, upon the ſpot, by Signor Lidarti, who lives there; Signor Gualberto Brunetti is Maeſtro di Capella at the cathedral; and Gherardeſchi, Renzini, Lidarti, and Corrucci, are eminent compoſers in that city.

At Perugia Signor Zanetti has long reſided; but he loſt his place of Maeſtro di Capella to the great church there, lately, by having appeared on the Aliberti ſtage at Rome, as a ſinger in an opera of his own compoſition, and that, merely to ſupply the place of the principal tenor, who had run away, and to prevent the piece from being ſtopt: he is ſince married to a pretty woman, who ſings well, and is likely to indemnify him for the loſs of his place.

At Parma, Signor Poncini is compoſer to the great church, as is Signor Colla to the prince; and Signor Ferrara, brother to the famous violin player, who is a remarkable fine performer on the violoncello; together with the celebrated ſinger Baſtardini, and Signora Roger, a great harpſichord player, who was miſtreſs to the princeſs of Aſturias, are all in penſion at the court of Parma. The theatre there is the largeſt in Europe; it is capable of containing four thouſand people, and has water under the ſtage ſufficient to form a great river, or for the repreſentation of a ſea-fight; but this theatre has not been uſed ſince the death of the laſt duke.

In arriving at Genoa, I found no other public musical performance than an *intermezzo*, in which Piatti, a young singer who had just returned from England, was principal.

From the number of musical establishments and performances mentioned in this journal, the Italians may, perhaps, be accused of cultivating music to excess; but whoever continues a short time in any of their principal cities, must perceive that other arts and sciences are not neglected: and even in travelling through the country, if the Ecclesiastical State be excepted, the natural fertility of the soil does not appear to be the only source of abundance in the necessaries of life; for I can venture to affirm, that, throughout Lombardy and Tuscany, agriculture is carried on with such art and activity, that I never remember to have seen lands better laid out, or less frequently suffered to lie idle: the poor, indeed, are oppresfed and rendered worthless by the rigour of government; but were they less so under their Gothic tyrants, when arts and sciences were not only neglected but extirpated from among them? Perhaps the cultivation of the peaceful arts may contribute as much to the happiness of the present inhabitants of Italy, and, indeed, of the rest of the world, as the conquering kingdoms did to that of their martial ancestors; who, when they were not busied in cutting the throats of each other, employed all their time and talents in plundering and enslaving mankind.

But music is now thought necessary in every country in Europe; and if it *must* be had, why should it not be excellent? The superior refinement of the Italian music cannot be fairly attributed to the great number of *artificial* voices with which Italy, to its dishonour, abounds; for vocal music seems at present in its highest state of perfection in the conservatorios of Venice, where only the *natural* voices of of females can be heard; ſo that the greateſt crime of which the Italians ſeem guilty is the having dared to apply to their ſofter language, a ſpecies of muſic more delicate and refined, than the reſt of Europe can boaſt.

It is now time to cloſe my account of the preſent ſtate of muſic in Italy, in doing which I cannot diſſemble my fears that the reader will think it prolix; as, upon reviſing my journal, I am ſorry to find that the further I advanced into that country, the more looſe is the texture of my narrative; for in proportion as I had more to hear and to ſee, I had leſs time to ſpare for reflection and for writing: indeed, the mere matters of fact concerning muſical exhibitions, will, I doubt, afford but ſmall entertainment to the reader; for they are ſo much the ſame, that an account of one is, in many particulars, an account of all; ſo that a circumſtantial narrative of things, perhaps not very intereſting in themſelves, might be

tireſome

tiresome even in spight of variety: all I have to urge in my defence, is, that the relation is faithful, and that, if the places, through which I passed had afforded more entertaining incidents, they would have been given to the public.

After a very fatiguing and dangerous journey over the tremendous mountains of Genoa, and through Provence and Languedoc, during incessant rains which had rendered the roads intolerable, I arrived at Lyons in my way home, Dec. 3d, where, in visiting the theatre, I was more disgusted than ever, at hearing French music, after the exquisite performances to which I had been accustomed in Italy. Eugenie, a pretty comedy, preceded Silvain, an opera by M. Gretry: there were many pretty passages in the music, but so ill sung, with so false an expression, such screaming, forcing, and trilling, as quite made me sick.

I tried to observe, on the road, by what degrees the French arrive at this extreme de-

depravity in their musical expression; and I find, that in descending the Alps, it does not come on all at once. In Provence and Languedoc, the tunes of the country people are rather pretty; I prevailed on them to sing me some wherever I stopt, which they did in a natural and simple manner. The airs are less wild than the Scots, as less ancient, but I rather think the melodies of Provence and Languedoc are older than any now subsisting that were formed upon the system of Guido.

From Lyons I travelled night and day to Paris, and arrived there on Saturday, Dec. 8th; but I shall detain my reader no longer with observations upon French music, of which the expression is notoriously hateful to all the people in Europe but themselves: however, in the midst of this seeming severity of decision, it is but just to own, that the French have as long known the mechanical laws of counter-point as any nation in Europe; and, that at present, by means of M. Rameau's system

and

and rules for a fundamental baſe, they are very good judges of harmony. It muſt likewiſe be allowed, that they have long been in poſſeſſion of ſimple and agreeable Provençale and Languedocian melodies, to which they continue to adapt the pretrieſt words, for ſocial purpoſes, of any people on the globe; and that they have now the merit of imitating very ſucceſsfully the muſic of the Italian burlettas, in their comic operas, and of greatly ſurpaſſing the Italians, and, perhaps, every other nation, in the poetical compoſition of thoſe dramas.

During my laſt reſidence at Paris, I had the honour of conferring with many men of letters of the firſt claſs, whoſe openneſs and politeneſs to me were ſuch as merit my moſt grateful and public acknowledgments; and I cannot reſiſt the deſire of mentioning two, among theſe, of a very diſtinguiſhed order, M. Diderot, and M. Rouſſeau.

With M. Diderot, I had the happineſs of converſing ſeveral times; and I was pleaſed to find, that among all the ſciences which his extenſive genius and learning have inveſtigated, there is no one that he intereſts himſelf more about, than muſic. Mademoiſelle Diderot, his daughter, is one of the fineſt harpſichord-players in Paris, and, for a lady, poſſeſſed of an uncommon portion of knowledge in modulation; but though I had the pleaſure of hearing her for ſeveral hours, not a ſingle French compoſition was played by her the whole time, all was Italian and German; hence it will not be difficult to form a judgment of M. Diderot's taſte in muſic. He entered ſo zealouſly into my views concerning the hiſtory of his favourite art, that he preſented me with a number of his own MSS. ſufficient for a volume in folio on the ſubject. Theſe, from ſuch a writer, I regard as invaluable; "Here, "take them, ſays he, I know not what "they contain; if any materials for your "purpoſe, uſe them in the courſe of

"your

"your work, as your own property; if "not, throw them into the fire." But notwithſtanding ſuch a legal transfer, I ſhall look upon myſelf as accountable for theſe papers, not only to M. Diderot, but to the public.

I regarded the meeting with M. Rouſſeau at Paris, as a ſingularly fortunate completion of my perſonal intercourſe with the learned and ingenious on the continent: I was ſo happy as to converſe for a conſiderable time with him upon muſic, a ſubject which has received ſuch embelliſhments from his pen, that the dryeſt parts of it are rendered intereſting by his manner of treating them, both in the Encyclopedie, and in his Muſical Dictionary. He read over my plan very attentively, and gave me his opinion of it, article by article; after which he made enquiries concerning ſeveral Italian compoſers of his acquaintance, and ſeemed to intereſt himſelf very much about the preſent ſtate of muſic in Italy, as well

well as the acquiſitions I had made there towards my future work.

* * * *

The reader of this journal will now be enabled not only to form an idea of the preſent ſtate of muſic in the countries through which I have paſſed, but likewiſe of the opportunities with which I have been favoured of conſulting the libraries and the learned, on whatever is moſt diſputable and curious in my projected hiſtory. I have mentioned ſome of the materials which I acquired, and to theſe may be added a great number, which I collected during many years in England, and near 400 volumes of ſcarce books on the ſubject of muſic, which I procured abroad. I have alſo ſettled a correſpondence in every great city that I viſited on the continent, by means of which I hope to be furniſhed from time to time with the neweſt intelligence concerning modern muſic, as well as with further

par-

particulars, relative to the ancient; and as I am certain that no place abounds more with men of ſound learning, or with collectors of curious compoſitions and valuable materials neceſſary to my intended work, than my own country; I humbly hope that I ſhall alſo be honoured with their counſel and communications.

But with all theſe requiſites, reſpect for the public, for the art about which I write, and even for myſelf, will prevent precipitate publication: a hiſtory of the kind I propoſe, muſt inevitably be a work of time; for after conſulting the moſt ſcarce and valuable books and MSS. and conferring with the moſt eminent artiſts and theoriſts; to ſelect, digeſt, and conſolidate materials ſo various and diffuſed, will not only require leiſure and labour, but ſuch a patient perſeverance, as little leſs than the zeal of enthuſiaſm can inſpire. It is not the hiſtory of an art in its infant ſtate, whoſe parents are ſtill

living,

living, that I have ventured to undertake; but one coeval with the world; one whose high antiquity renders its origin as doubtful, as the formation of language, or the first articulations of the human voice.

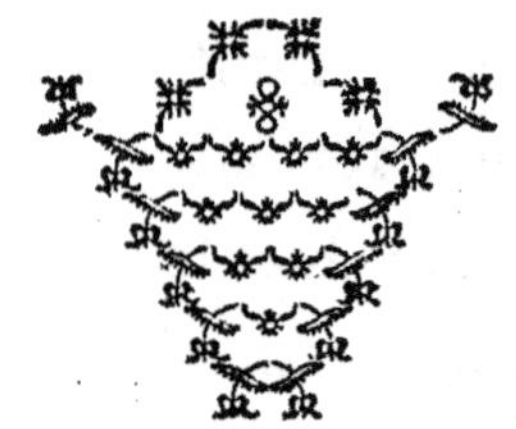

INDEX.

Bocchirini,

INDEX.

Conti,

I N D E X.

INDEX.

Rota,

I N D E X.

F I N I S.

ADVERTISEMENT.

A General Plan of the author's intended Hiſtory of Muſic, *with Propoſals for Printing it by Subſcription, will be ſubmitted to the public as ſoon as the work is ſufficiently advanced to enable him to fix a time with any degree of certainty for its appearance.*

Titles published by Travis & Emery:

www.ingramcontent.com/pod-product-compliance
Lightning Source LLC
Chambersburg PA
CBHW060236100426
42742CB00011B/1549

* 9 7 8 1 9 0 4 3 3 1 7 6 6 *